# The Jewish Dream Book

## The Key to Opening the Inner Meaning of Your Dreams

Vanessa L. Ochs
with Elizabeth Ochs
Illustrated by Kristina Swarner

For People of All Faiths, All Backgrounds
Jewish Lights Publishing
Woodstock, Vermont

*The Jewish Dream Book:*
*The Key to Opening the Inner Meaning of Your Dreams*

2003 First Printing
Text © 2003 by Vanessa L. Ochs with Elizabeth Ochs
Illustrations © 2003 by Kristina Swarner

For information regarding permission to reprint material from this book, please mail or fax your request in writing to Jewish Lights Publishing, Permissions Department, at the address / fax number listed below, or e-mail your request to permissions@jewishlights.com.

**Library of Congress Cataloging–in–Publication Data**
Ochs, Vanessa L.
The Jewish dream book : the key to opening the inner meaning of your dreams / Vanessa L. Ochs with Elizabeth Ochs; illustrations by Kristina Swarner.
     p. cm.
Includes bibliographical references.
ISBN 1-58023-132-2 (pbk.)
1. Dreams—Religious aspects—Judaism. 2. Dream interpretation. 3. Dream interpretation in rabbinical literature. I. Ochs, Elizabeth, 1984– II. Title.
BF1078.O24 2003
296.7'1—dc21

2003006452

10  9  8  7  6  5  4  3  2  1

Manufactured in Malaysia

*For People of All Faiths, All Backgrounds*
Published by Jewish Lights Publishing
A Division of LongHill Partners, Inc.
Sunset Farm Offices, Route 4, P.O. Box 237
Woodstock, VT 05091
Tel: (802) 457–4000        Fax: (802) 457–4004
www.jewishlights.com

For Julie and Peter

# Contents

# Acknowledgments

Special thanks to our wonderful editor, Donna Zerner, and to our many friends at Jewish Lights Publishing.

# Introduction

You have before you a bedside companion, drawn from ancient and modern Jewish texts and traditions that may help you better understand your dreams and enrich your life.

Perhaps you have been thinking about dreams for some time now, contemplating the insights they might hold and reveal. If you have been studying dream interpretation in diverse cultures or from a variety of psychological perspectives, you would be absolutely correct to surmise, "Surely a tradition both as ancient and as adaptive to modernity as Judaism must offer worthwhile insights into the nature of dreaming and dream interpretation." It is that information you have before you.

Know for sure that there is no such thing as *the* Jewish approach to dreaming. Judaism, thousands of years old, holds within it the collected wisdom of many sacred texts, many scholars, and the experiences of many men and women who have lived in different places and have studied, practiced, and transmitted Judaism in creative ways. Thus, you will find a range of teachings and practices.

This book will help you explore and honor your own dreams by engaging in Jewish dream practices that are rooted in antiquity and have been updated in light of contemporary understandings about dreaming. The book is organized into two parts. The first part presents an overview of Jewish teachings on dreams and dream interpretation. The second part offers a variety of dream practices with sufficient instructions to help you perform them. The concluding section of the book contains a selection of resources for further study as you proceed beyond this introductory guide.

We hope that in your own study and spiritual practice you will discover Jewish ways of having a dream life that is rich in insight and leads to spiritual growth.

# How This Book Came to Be Written

I (Vanessa) share the story of how this book came to be written because, in part, it may parallel your own journey.

For a long time, much of my knowledge about what Judaism had to teach about dreams came from *Fiddler on the Roof*, with spirits of the dead appearing in dreams and bearing threats and predictions, folk beliefs of my great-grandmother's world that I had sloughed off in favor of more rational thinking. Despite having rich exposure to Judaism in family life and academic study, I didn't see resources for illumination in my own life when I thought about Jews and dreams.

Although I knew the important biblical dream sequences, I didn't see them as resources for my own spiritual life. The dreams that made the most impression on me back in Hebrew school days were about Jacob and his dream of angels going up and down a ladder, and of Joseph and his dreams of dominating his brothers and his interpretations of Pharaoh's dreams. However engaging the stories, I didn't connect the male dreamers or the male dream interpreters of the Bible to my own dream life.

Biblical dreams didn't inspire me to seek out Jewish resources on dreaming that could help me dream as a Jew or interpret my own dreams in Jewish ways. I never imagined I might have dreams that held visions within them, or that I

*(Sholem Aleichem's Tevye the dairyman pretends to wake up in the middle of the night from a terrible dream in order to convince his wife that their daughter should marry the tailor she loves, and not the old butcher whom the matchmaker has selected.)*

*"Oh my God, Tevye," she says, "you're delirious. It was only a dream. Spit three times against the Evil Eye, tell me what you dreamed, and you'll see that it's nothing to be afraid of."*

*"I'll tell you my dream. But*

might work to discern God's presence in my dream world. Dreams came under the part of my life that I thought of as "private," not subject to Jewish laws or teachings.

Would I have thought otherwise if the Bible recorded descriptions of important women dreamers? Had I read that God appeared to Sarah in her dream and told her to set off on a journey to a land of promise, I might have begun listening for the divine voice in my own dreams long ago. As it stands, God appeared only to Abraham in a dream and in visions, which set Abraham off on his journey to become the father of a great nation. Sarah is depicted as the wife who, along with the livestock, tags along.

Fortunately, I, like many others, have been inspired by the work of feminist biblical scholars, and have learned to read Jewish sacred texts in more expansive ways so that I can feel that the words include both women and men. I have learned to imagine the words God spoke to Sarah in her dreams, words that were never recorded. I have imagined dreams given to the other women in the Bible that prompted them to set forth on their own spiritual paths.

I also learned that there is no part of life that cannot be shaped and made sacred through Judaism—including dreams. As one who analyzes and develops new Jewish rituals, I have learned how to study practices performed by Jews in different settings, ancient and modern, in order to adapt them to our lives today.

Ultimately, it was the study of a particular volume of the Babylonian Talmud (the multivolume compendium of Jewish law and lore dating back to the period between 200–500 C.E.) that most deeply revealed to me that Judaism had a great deal to teach about dreams and dreaming that could be integrated into one's life. (Talmud study among Jewish women is a fairly

*I'll have to ask you, Golde, to control yourself and not panic, because our holy books say that no dream can come true more than 75 percent, and that the rest of it is pure poppycock, such stuff and nonsense that only a fool would believe in…and now listen. At first I dreamed that we were having some sort of celebration, a wedding or engagement party…. Then a door opened and in came your Grandmother Tsaytl, God rest her soul….*

*(Tsaytl congratulates them, pleased to hear her great-granddaughter is marrying the tailor, and not the butcher she's been matched with. Then the butcher's dead wife, Frume Soreh, appears bearing threats. Tevye tells the next part of his dream.)*

*"Frume Soreh grabbed me by the throat and began to squeeze so hard that if you hadn't waked me when you did, I'd be in the world to come now."*

*"Tfu! Tfu! Tfu!" Goes my wife, spitting three times…. "And if my grandmother, may she rest in peace, has taken the trouble of coming all the way from the next world to wish us a mazal tov, we'd better say mazal tov ourselves…."*

Sholem Aleichem[1]

new phenomenon, one chronicled in my book *Words on Fire.* Only in the last two decades have many women even had the opportunity, let alone the linguistic skills, to read these texts that form the bedrock of Jewish belief and practice.) I was studying the volume of the Talmud called *Brakhot,* meaning "blessings." I learned that long after biblical dreamers such as Abraham and Joseph, who saw their dreams as encounters with God, and long before modern dream interpreters such as Freud and Jung, who saw dreams as insights into the unconscious mind, the best Jewish minds of antiquity were putting their heads together to make sense of dreaming. In the Talmudic period, dreams were considered a particular category of blessing, a gift that had to be opened in order to discern its blessing: instructions on how to better live one's life or hints about what the future might hold. In *Brakhot,* the patchwork of insights into dreaming constitute a little "book of dreams," comparable to the dream books of other traditions, both ancient and contemporary, offering both a general understanding about the nature of dreams and a manual for how to interpret dream imagery.

What serious attention the ancient Rabbis paid to their own dreams—so serious that their discussions merited inclusion in the Talmud, this compilation of sacred conversations across the generations! The Rabbis were not the only ones concerned about dreams. In addition to approaching their rabbis with questions about whether pots were kosher or how to observe Passover, ordinary men and women brought dreams to their rabbis (whose job description included dream interpretation) as well as to a group of ritual experts called dream interpreters. (How similar this is to the way contemporary people bring dreams to therapists.) Ancient dreamers, both rabbis and laypeople, had many of the same questions we still

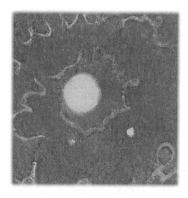

*Once Joseph had a dream that he told to his brothers, which made them hate him even more. He told them, "Hear this dream which I have dreamed: We were binding sheaves in the field, when suddenly my sheaf stood up and remained upright. Then your sheaves gathered around and bowed low to my sheaf." His brothers answered, "Do you intend to rule over us?" And they hated him even more for his talk about his dreams.*

(Genesis 37:5–8)

have about dreams. What does Jewish tradition have to say about the dream that I just had? How do I discern the voice of God in the curious assemblage of dream images that visit me in the night? If I had a nightmare, how can Judaism help me make sense of it and cope with the horrible feeling it has given me?

From the texts we have inherited, we can see that the sages of the Talmud, whose words help Jews live every single moment of their lives in sacred Jewish ways, appeared to believe there were distinctive ways we could go about sleeping, dreaming, waking, and thinking about our dreams. How moving to see the diverse ways the rabbis answered the questions brought to them about dreaming, affirming that Jewish tradition has long been capable of holding a wide range of perspectives. It struck me: if we paid as much attention to our own dreams as the sages and the Jews of antiquity paid to theirs, couldn't we also experience our dreams as blessings, divine gifts of instruction and even of healing?

In *Brakhot* and elsewhere, I continued to study the Talmudic passages on dreams, first on my own, and then with my daughter Elizabeth, who was in high school at the time. She, too, was beguiled by the passages on dreams. (Having previously studied only those parts of Talmud that concerned matters of Jewish law, Elizabeth was delighted to discover a whole other face of Talmud, one that addressed her spiritual life.) We'd wake up in the morning and, over our Cheerios, would talk through our dreams with a Jewish consciousness, helping each other go beyond our dreams' quirkiness and discover in them signs of wisdom and guidance.

For her friend's birthday, Elizabeth made a handmade book of whimsical collages based on the texts on dreams we had studied, thus making the Talmudic Jewish teachings on

*As the sun was about to set, a deep sleep fell upon Abram, and a great dark dread descended upon him. And God said to Abram, "Know for certain that your offspring shall be strangers in a land not their own, and they shall be enslaved and oppressed for four hundred years. But I will execute judgment on the nation they serve, and afterwards they shall go free with great wealth. As for you, you shall go to your fathers in peace and you shall be buried at a ripe old age."*

(Genesis 15:12–15)

dreams accessible for her friend Jesse. Watching Elizabeth create that book and seeing the delight and interest it inspired led me to invite her to collaborate with me on this book, which draws on a wide range of Jewish teachings and practices and emphasizes the Talmudic teachings on dreams that so inspired us. Elizabeth has assisted with research and written a number of the sections. Kristina Swarner, an artist beloved by us both for her elegant and fanciful dream-evoking imagery, joins us; we are honored to work with her.

*"If you see a white horse, either moving at a gentle trot or galloping, something good will happen to you"* (*Babylonian Talmud,* Brakhot 56b).

# part 1

# What Judaism Teaches Us about Dreaming

# The Origin of Dreams

The ancient Jewish sages' wisdom about dreams and their interpretation anticipated the theories and practices of dream interpretation we now link to that modern Jew who took dreams so seriously, Sigmund Freud, the father of psychoanalysis. Freud certainly made use of the Jewish texts he was likely to have studied as a boy. To be sure, in his dream interpretations, he relied upon the Jewish practice of digging deeply to interpret words and experiences (found not just in sacred texts, but in the story one told about one's own life) in order to find meaning and achieve self-understanding. In a Freudian reading of dreams and in a Jewish reading of sacred texts, there is never a single, clear meaning. Rather, layers of meaning are always being disclosed and multiple meanings are always possible.

Before we explore essential Jewish teachings about dreams, we first need to understand what a dream is and to consider why we dream.

# What Happens When We Dream?

Sleep is altogether central to our lives. We spend approximately one-third of our lives sleeping and we dream for one-quarter of that time period. There are two different kinds of sleep: NREM sleep and REM sleep. The first, otherwise known as Non-Rapid Eye Movement sleep, occupies around 75 percent of our sleeping hours. This is when our blood pressure and heart rate decrease. The second, known as Rapid Eye Movement sleep, occupies around 25 percent of our sleeping hours and is what we normally call dreaming. As we sleep, our minds undergo an alternating cycle of NREM sleep and REM sleep. During REM sleep, our heart rate increases, our blood pressure fluctuates, and, as the name implies, our eyes oscillate quickly beneath our eyelids. On average, we experience five cycles of REM sleep a night, ranging from 15 to 60 minutes. REM sleep is 50 percent of newborns' sleep, 25 percent of adolescents' and adults' sleep, and 18 percent of elderly people's sleep.

# Why Do We Dream?

Amost every scholar, scientist, psychologist, and spiritual leader has his or her own explanation as to why we dream. Some believe that dreaming enables us to process the experiences of our day and make sense of our lives. Others support the hypothesis that people dream in order to solve problems that their conscious mind could not resolve during the day. Some take a biological angle: dreaming enables the nervous system to dispose of unnecessary memories and stimulates the developing mind. Recent research suggests that dreaming supplies the corneas of our eyes with much needed oxygen. Although some people firmly support one understanding of dreaming above all others, most people incorporate several hypotheses into their personal dream explanations.

# Where Do Dreams Come From?

Jewish teachings are divided about the origin of dreams. Some focus on the divine origin of our dreams; others focus on the human origin of dreams. We see evidence of both perspectives in early and later sources.

## The Divine Origin of Dreams

The divine origin of dreams is demonstrated in the story of Joseph, the most famous dreamer and dream interpreter. He is a third-generation dreamer. It was his father, Jacob, who encountered God through a dream of a ladder with ascending and descending angels; Joseph's grandfather, Abraham, experienced affirmation that he would be the father of a great nation through a dream. One can imagine that the members of that family were trained to discern God's presence in their dreams and were not surprised to be chosen as vessels through which God's will was made known in dreams. Significantly, they didn't hesitate to act upon dream messages they received.

As a young man, Joseph has a dream of his brothers' sheaves of wheat bowing down to his sheaf; another of the sun, moon, and eleven planets bowing down to him. These dreams are interpreted to indicate that Joseph is fated to rule over his brothers. Although the interpretations are indeed accurate, sharing these dreams only make his brothers hate him more.

Imprisoned in the court of Pharaoh, Joseph finds his way to freedom through accurate interpretations of the dreams of fellow prisoners, the cupbearer and the baker. Encountering the men, he notices from their demeanor how sad they are, even before they reveal their troubling dreams that require interpretation. Thus, in this second set of dreams, we see that Joseph is already engaging in dream interpretation that reflects his growing social maturity.

*And they (the cupbearer and baker) said to him, "We had dreams, and there is no one to interpret them." So Joseph said to them, "Surely God can interpret! Tell me your dreams."*

(Genesis 40:8)

Joseph now sees that it is God who gives dreams and God who gives him the gift of correct and timely interpretation. When the baker is released from prison, as Joseph predicts he will be, the baker recommends Joseph to Pharaoh as an interpreter after Pharaoh fails to find a satisfying interpretation for two of his own dreams.

Joseph hears Pharaoh's dreams, one concerning seven healthy cows being consumed by seven scrawny cows, and the other concerning seven ears of healthy grain swallowing up seven ears of thin, scorched grain. Not only does Joseph see that these dreams predict seven years of plenty followed by seven years of famine, but he also convinces Pharaoh to prepare for the years of famine. Joseph sees God's hand in the dreams and in his own capacity to interpret them: "As for Pharaoh having had the same dream twice, it means that the matter has been determined by God, and that God will carry it out" (Genesis 41:32). A dream interpreter now at his peak, Joseph does the sacred work of world repair, improving upon the future, which is even more important than predicting it.

Other biblical dreamers who experience the Divine in their dreams include Samuel and Solomon (called to holy missions as was Abraham), and Daniel, who interprets dreams that will foretell the future. The prophets, too, hear God's voice through the medium of dreams and receive divine messages that will sustain the Jewish people, particularly through exile. As we read of God's desire in Jeremiah: "Let the prophet who has a dream tell the dream; and let him who has received My word report My word faithfully" (Jeremiah 23:28).

Just as the prophets encounter God through their dreams, we, through our own dreams, can have a tiny taste of the prophetic experience. As the Talmud teaches, "a dream is one-sixtieth part of prophecy." The *Zohar*, the book of Jewish

*Pharaoh said to Joseph, "I have had a dream but no one can interpret it. But I have heard it that you need only hear a dream to tell its meaning." Joseph answered Pharaoh, "It is God who will give Pharaoh an answer of peace."*

(Genesis 41:15–16)

*Five things are a sixtieth of something else: fire, honey, Sabbath, sleep, and a dream.*

*Fire is one-sixtieth part of Gehinnom.*

*Honey is one-sixtieth part of manna.*

*Sabbath is one-sixtieth part of the world to come.*

*Sleep is one-sixtieth part of death.*

*A dream is one-sixtieth part of prophecy.*

(Babylonian Talmud, Brakhot 57b)

*Nothing takes place in the world except that which was previously made known, either through a dream or through a proclamation. It has been affirmed that before any event comes to pass in the world, it is first announced in heaven, from where it is proclaimed to the world. As it is written in Amos (3:7), "Indeed, my Lord God does nothing without having revealed God's purpose to God's servants, the prophets." This refers to a time when there were still prophets in the world. When the prophets ceased, the sages succeeded them. In our time, when the wise sages are no longer with us, that which is to come is revealed in dreams.*

(*Zohar* I:183b)

mysticism, expresses a belief that in a world in which there are no longer prophets and no longer even wise sages, divine wisdom is revealed to *us* through dreams.

The *Zohar* acknowledges that not all dreams contain the voice of God. Whereas the righteous, connected to the higher realms, may hear prophecy in their dreams, the sinners do not.

Those who believe that in dreams, we, too, can still hear God's voice, believe that in our divinely inspired dreams God reaches out to us, offering us healing, comfort, teaching, wisdom, and assistance as we make decisions and anticipate future events. Dreams are messages, a way in which God approaches us and in which we apprehend God. Those holding such a perspective distinguish between dreams that are divine communication and dreams that reflect only our preoccupations with the daily world.

Some people believe that all of human experience, the unfolding of God's creation, is God's dream. The belief that everything that happens in the world is God's dream is reflected in the writings of Edmond Jabes:

> *Do you not remember this phrase of Reb Alsem's: "We live out the dream of creation, which is God's dream. Evenings, our own dreams snuggle down into it like sparrows in their nests"?*
>
> *And did not Reb Hames write: "Birds of night, my dreams explore the immense dream of the sleeping universe"?*
>
> Edmond Jabes[2]

# The Human Origin of Dreams

Other Jewish sages caution us *not* to attempt to communicate with God in our dreams, *not* to jump to the conclusion that through our dreams, we have communicated with God. Human consciousness, they claim, is at play in the fabrication of dreams. Accordingly, our dreams come from our imaginations. They are woven from the thoughts that are already in our minds and hearts, and uncover matters that we are already dwelling upon, consciously or unconsciously.

Two explanations for a perspective that resists seeing God's hand in dreams come to mind. The first is the age-old Jewish anxiety about people who engage in spiritual practices in which they relinquish control to achieve closeness to God. (This is one reason why the early Hasidim, proponents of ecstatic singing and dancing as part of prayer, encountered so much opposition.) Taking one's dreams seriously, like engaging in mystical contemplation, is considered a problematic spiritual technology by which one gives oneself up to sacred experience; it is an altered state of consciousness. Most Jewish leaders have tended to prefer a safer, more predictable and rational Jewish path, proposing that one encounter God through regular communal prayer, study of Torah, and performance of *mitzvot* (commandments) and acts of lovingkindness (such as feeding the poor and caring for the elderly). Claim a connection to God through direct experience and people worry about you; absorb yourself in the pursuit of dreams and you'll be called, derogatorily, "a dreamer," criticized for taking time and energy away from study and deeds.

The second explanation emerges from devastating episodes in Jewish history. There are recorded accounts of individuals who pointed to their dreams in order to claim that they were prophets, even messiahs, and gained some acceptance because people so despaired of their lot. To prevent a repeat of catastrophic disappointments and embarrassing hoaxes, Jews have been taught not to look at our own dreams or anyone else's as evidence of prophetic experience. Be suspicious of people who make haughty claims about God's presence in their dreams. Stay away from those who use dreams as a form of divination (that is, attempting to control God's will or force the hand of God) or who point to their dreams to affirm that God has vested authority in them.

Such prejudice against the dreamer has roots in the Bible. In Deuteronomy, the Israelites are warned, "If there appears among you a prophet or diviner of dreams and you are given a sign or a portent saying, 'Let us follow and worship another god'—whom you have not experienced—do not heed the words of that prophet or dream diviner. For the Lord God is testing you…" (Deuteronomy 13:2–4). Indeed, the evil dream-diviner is to be put to death! In Jeremiah, we learn that God despises the false prophet who makes claims about dream revelations: "I have heard what the prophets say, who prophesy falsely in My name: 'I had a dream, I had a dream.' How long will there be in the minds of the prophets who prophesy falsehood…who plan to make My people forget My name, by means of dreams which they tell each other…" (Jeremiah 23:25–27).

Even in this perspective favoring the human construction of dreams, God is not taken out of the picture altogether, for God has given us the dreaming mind and the capacity to see and remember the images of our dreams.

*"A dream that is not interpreted is like a letter that is not opened"* (*Babylonian Talmud*, Brakhot 55a).

# chapter two

# Classical Jewish Approaches to Dream Interpretation

One assertion about dreams has resonance for most Jewish sages: a dream invites interpretation. This often-quoted aphorism tells it all: "A dream that is not interpreted is like a letter that is not opened" (Babylonian Talmud, *Brakhot* 55a).

*An uninterpreted dream is like a letter that is not opened.* The metaphor is a rich one. Consider some of a letter's characteristics. It is a message that comes from outside ourselves. It travels a distance and arrives nearby without any effort on our part: we are passive recipients. It does not come to us as an object we have worked for or crafted, but as a potential gift. It accosts us, making its way across the threshold of our consciousness. Typically we do not know what is inside, and we may be beguiled by its mystery. As soon as we open it, the suspense is over and the mystery is solved. The

*There was once a woman who came to Rabbi Eleazear so he could interpret her dream.*

*She told him, "I dreamt that the beam of my house was split."*

*He told her, "You will give birth to a son."*

*She departed, and it happened just as he predicted.*

*Once again, she came to Rabbi Eleazear.*

*This time, she told him, "I dreamt that the beam of my house was split."*

*Once again, he told her, "You will give birth to a son."*

*She departed, and once again, it happened just as he predicted.*

*She came to Rabbi Eleazear a third time.*

*This time, she found all of his students were assembled in their school, but Rabbi Eleazear, their teacher, was not there.*

*She asked his students, "Where is your teacher?"*

*They asked her, "What do you want of him?"*

contents, once absorbed, are potentially transformative.

Comparing a dream to a letter, the Rabbis teach that a dream is a gift, an opportunity that comes in the form of a message to be deciphered. Should we fail to discern the meaning of our dreams, we refuse to learn information that could have transformed our lives, even the world. Fail to open up our dreams, and we may lose the opportunity to make bold decisions, to fight for what we believe in, to make difficult but important changes, or to set forth on new journeys with wisdom and self-understanding. Fail to unpack a dream and be changed by its message, and we resist transformation; we resist being moved.

The sages believed that all dreams "follow the mouth," meaning that the significance of a dream does not rest in the dream itself, but in interpretations emerging from the dream. How does one access the meaning, open up the dream? In the Talmudic world, ideally, one has it interpreted by someone who is gifted in this art.

The sages make clear that there is not a single correct interpretation that emerges from each dream. In fact, a person may consult with many interpreters and receive many different interpretations, and all of them might be true, each in its own way.

Dream interpreters can alter reality, according to scholar Ken Frieden.[1] There is a story in the Talmud about Bar Hedya, an interpreter of dreams, who gives positive interpretations to those who pay him and negative interpretations to those who don't. Rava, who never pays Bar Hedya, receives only negative interpretations, and they are all fulfilled. Rava finally starts paying Bar Hedya and suddenly his dreams are favorably interpreted. When Rava dreams that his house collapses and everyone comes and takes bricks, Bar Hedya tells him,

"Your teaching will be disseminated through the world."

When Rava finally understands the system, he chastises and curses Bar Hedya: "You wicked man! It was all fulfilled through your hand and you gave me all this pain." The Talmud, however, does not jump in with critique, as one might expect, exposing Bar Hedya as a phony. In fact, this story becomes an opportunity to teach the importance of paying any healer for services rendered, recalled in the adage, "One who charges nothing is worth nothing." (Ultimately, however, Bar Hedya does meet an untimely fate.)

Some dreams, more than others, call out for interpretation. According to the Talmud, a dream that wakes one up or that occurs near the morning demands interpretation, as does a dream that leaves one feeling sad. The interpreter plays a role in relieving anguish and alleviating the distress of such dreams. "The Jewish dream interpreter," rabbi and psychologist Joel Covitz writes, "was like a sacred technician who probed the dream in order to extract from it the particular will or destiny that God wanted for the dreamer. The interpreter would not simply acknowledge the message of the dream but would actively formulate and recommend a solution to the dreamer's problem as expressed in the dream."[2]

# Jewish Approaches to Interpreting Dream Symbols

The dreams a culture deems "good" reinforce the values of that culture. Thus, there can be no such thing as a universal code of dream interpretation, because each culture manipulates symbols differently. For the Jewish sages, a "good" dream might involve images that can be understood as representing the study of Torah; having a strong and healthy family life;

*She answered, "Perhaps you are as wise as your teacher and you can interpret my dream?"*

*They told her, "Tell us your dream and we will interpret it."*

*She told them, "I dreamt that the beam of my house was split."*

*They replied, "You will bury your husband."*

*When she left the students, she began to cry.*

*Rabbi Eleazear, who had just returned, asked his students, "Why is this woman crying?"*

*The students answered, "She came looking for you, but you were not here."*

*Rabbi Eleazear asked them, "Why did she come?"*

*"So you could interpret her dream."*

*"And what did you tell her?" he asked.*

*The students told him what they had said.*

*He told them, "You have killed a man, for as it is taught, 'A dream follows its interpretation.'"*

(Adapted from Midrash Rabbah on Lamentations)

leading a virtuous life; being embraced by a solid community; and having enough peace, safety, heath, and financial resources to make all of the above possible. When the sages interpreted the dream symbols of their time and their culture, they transmitted and reinforced, consciously or not, the values by which their communities lived. Their interpretations must have felt logical, even obvious, to them.

It's worth noting that most of the interpretation of dream symbols in the Talmudic period was intended to predict something that was going to happen so that one could anticipate or prepare for it. This is, of course, distinct from the modern, psychological perspective in which dream symbols are seen as revelatory of some aspect of our psyche.

The ancient interpretive strategies that continue to make the most sense to us are the ones whose symbols still evoke similar feelings. For instance, the rabbis saw the dream image of a horse gently trotting into the horizon as a sign of good things to come, an image we, too, can grasp. Other interpretations may seem too rooted in the experiences of antiquity for us to access. If the sight of a donkey once inspired feelings of salvation ("If you see a donkey in a dream, you will be saved," Babylonian Talmud, *Brakhot*), it no longer does (except, perhaps, for Democrats).

By studying the Talmudic dream interpretations we have selected below, both those that we can relate to and even those that no longer speak to us, we can learn about the ancient Jewish world and discern what they valued. We can also train ourselves to get into the habit of looking for the symbolic meanings that lie inside our own dreams. (We have omitted some interpretations based on word play that depend upon an understanding of the particular language of biblical verses and those that hinge on a connection between the dream imagery

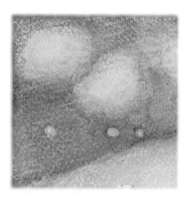

*For God speaks to us,*
*time and again,*

*When we are deeply sleeping,*

*Though we may not perceive it*
*as God's voice.*

*In a dream, in a night vision,*

*When we are deeply sleeping,*

*When we slumber in our beds.*

*Then God opens up our*
*understanding,*

*Teaching us, leaving a divine*
*mark.*

(Adapted from Job 33:14–17)

or language and biblical verses.) You may wish to compile your own private directory of dream images and the symbolic meanings they hold for you as a reference guide. (I know that for me, a dream about the first day of class means I am anxious about something that's about to happen, even if it's not school-related. Usually I'm worried about performing in new situations or being prepared for the unexpected.)

# Talmudic Interpretations of Dream Symbols

We have arranged this sampler of Talmudic interpretations of dream symbols according to a variety of topics including animals, food, and places and situations. Can these ancient interpretations help you unlock the meanings of your own dreams?

## Dreams about Animals

If an ox kicks you in your dream, a long journey awaits you.

If you eat an ox in a dream, you will become wealthy.

If there is a cat in your dream, a beautiful song is being composed for you.

If you see a male chicken, you will have a son.

If there is a hen in your dream, you will have a beautiful garden and a reason to rejoice.

If you see a young donkey standing near your head and braying, you will become a king or the head of a school.

If you see a goose in your dream, you will become wise.

If you see an elephant in your dream, wonders will be performed for you.

If you see a white horse, either moving at a gentle trot or galloping, something good will happen to you.

*Dreams are full of unexpressed fears and hopes, things we never even think of consciously. We think of them unconsciously deep down inside ourselves, and they come out in dreams. They don't always come out straight, though. Sometimes they come out in symbols. You have to learn to interpret the symbols.*

Chaim Potok[3]

If you see a goat, you will have many blessings in the coming year. If you see many goats, you will have many years of blessing.

If you see a snake, you will make a good living.

## Dreams about Food

If you see wheat in your dream, peace will follow you throughout your life.

If you see gourds in your dream, it means you fear heaven with all your might.

If you see barley in your dream, your sins will be forgiven.

If you see a branch of a vine, you can expect to greet the Messiah.

If you see a fig in your dream, you will remember all you have learned.

A pomegranate in your dream increases three things: your business, your knowledge, and your good deeds.

If you see olive trees, you will have many children.

If you see an olive, you will have a good name.

If you see olive trees in your dream, you will be blessed with abundance.

If you see olive oil, you may hope for the light of Torah.

If you see an egg and it breaks, your dream will be fulfilled.

## Dreams about Places and Situations in Which You Find Yourself

If you are in chains in your dream, you will be protected.

If you see a eulogy written in your dream, you will be spared and redeemed.

Three dreams foretell peace: a river, a bird, and a kettle.

*Since dreamers themselves are unaware of the meaning of the symbols they use, it is difficult at first sight to discover the source of the connection between the symbols and what they replace and represent.... For with the help of a knowledge of dream symbolism, it is possible to understand the meaning of separate elements of the content of a dream.... Here we are... returning to the technique of interpretation used by the ancients, to whom dream interpretation was identical with interpretation by means of symbols.*

Sigmund Freud[4]

If you see a well in your dream, you will behold peace and become a great Torah scholar.

If you go up on the roof in your dream, you will rise to prominence.

If you enter into a large town in your dream, your desires will be fulfilled.

If you enter a marsh in your dream, you will be the head of a school.

If you are sitting on a small boat in your dream, you will gain a good reputation.

It is a good omen to cut your hair in a dream.

If the walls of your house collapse in your dream, you will acquire boundless property.

If your house falls and everyone comes to take away the bricks, your teachings will spread throughout the world.

If your nose falls off, you will stop feeling so angry.

If you see a reed in your dream, you will become wise.

If you see yourself on a small boat, you will have a good reputation. If you see yourself on a big boat, your entire family will be well respected.

If you see yourself wearing *tefillin* (prayer straps) in your dream, you will rise to greatness.

If you see yourself praying in a dream, that is a good sign.

If you see a *lulav* (palm branch, myrtle, and willow) or an *etrog* (citron) in your dream, you are especially beloved by God.

If you see King David, you will become pious. If you see King Solomon, you will become wise.

If you see the Book of Esther, a miracle will be performed for you.

(Adapted from Babylonian Talmud, *Brakhot* 55a–57a)

# part 2
# Jewish Dream Practices

*The following anthology of Jewish dream practices is meant as a resource for you to adapt to your own life and needs. You can choose to use them just as they are presented, or you can view them as sources of inspiration as you sculpt your own dream practices. Feel free to find meaningful linkages between the Jewish practices and the effective dream practices you may have learned about in other settings—cultural, spiritual, or therapeutic.*

*Most of these dream practices stem from* minhagim, *or customs, both old and new, which frees us to be creative and inventive. That is to say, with the exception of one ritual held during the Torah service that honors those who are working with dreams, they are not tied to halakhah, Jewish law.*

*To reflect upon your dreams,*
*you need to remember them.*

# chapter three

# Bedtime Rituals to Help Prepare for Dreaming

The traditional Jewish bedtime ritual is a collection of prayers that many people learn in an abbreviated fashion early in childhood as they hear their parents recite the *Sh'ma* prayer for them until they can learn to sing it for themselves. For both adults and children, this bedtime ritual expresses gratitude for the day that has passed and creates a passageway from the waking state into a meaningful dream life. Certain dream practices can be appended to the traditional Jewish bedtime prayers and can serve to deepen your spiritual preparation for dreaming. They include placing a *sefer chalomot* (dream book) by your bed and engaging in *cheshbon hanefesh,* or reflection (taking an inventory of your soul).

After a period of saying the Jewish bedtime prayers and engaging in some of the bedtime dream practices, we hope you will discover that you are guiding your spirit to remember your dreams and to attend to the divine messages held within them.

## *Sefer Chalomot:* Book of Dreams

To reflect upon your dreams, you need to remember them. That's a problem if your dreams tend to slip away as soon as you wake up. This problem can have a simple solution. Sometimes all you need to do to recall your dreams is to *commit* yourself to remembering them, saying to yourself before you go to bed, "I will recall my dreams!"

But like a medicine that starts to work only after a while, this practice can take a few weeks of intending to remember before you actually do. If you grow impatient before you start being able to recall your dreams, we suggest the following approach, which is a jump-start to remembering dreams.

First, select a *sefer chalomot,* a dream book. For example, this can be a journal devoted to recording your dreams. Pick a journal with a cover and pages that appeal to you and evoke some of the feelings you have about the world of dreams. You might choose to design your own book cover with collages of dreams you recall or images that appear dreamlike to you. (The dream journal Elizabeth made for her friend Jesse is decorated throughout with quotes from the Talmud about dreams and with collages of dream images clipped from magazines, cards, and beautiful tea-bag envelopes.) If a fancy journal inhibits you, leave plain paper by your bedside and collect the sheets in a folder or binder. For many people, a dream book works best when they plan to record their dreams on one page and leave the facing page free for interpretations. Whether you use a journal or single sheets of paper, select blank unlined pages so that you can feel as unrestrained as possible.

*Laying in bed just before you go to sleep and reviewing your day can help center your thoughts and encourage enlightening, productive dreams.*

Place your *sefer chalomot* right next to your bed so you can reach it without getting up. Even a journey of a few steps to your dresser can dislodge your dreams from your mind.

## *Cheshbon Hanefesh:* Taking an Inventory of Your Soul

Lying in bed just before you go to sleep and reviewing your day can help center your thoughts and encourage enlightening, productive dreams. This reflective activity is called *cheshbon hanefesh,* "taking an inventory of your soul." It's a mini-version of the self-inspection Jews do in the days between Rosh Hashanah (the New Year) and Yom Kippur (the Day of Atonement), when we reflect back on the life we have led during the past year and review it analytically before we move into a new year. Jews believe that after one takes stock, changing one's ways is possible. The process is called *teshuvah,* "turning." It may involve not only planning new paths for oneself but also seeking forgiveness from individuals one has hurt and from God.

This is important spiritual work, and it is a pity that most people turn to this primary Jewish resource of reflection, self-inspection, and seeking forgiveness only one time a year, when we could be doing it every night. (In fact, you may find that if you fast on Yom Kippur, you are too light-headed to be properly introspective.) In a nightly *cheshbon hanefesh,* consider the following:

- What happened today?
- Whom did you encounter?
- What were some of the different feelings you experienced?
- What did you feel proud of?
- What do you wish you could improve upon?

*(A famous* sefer chalomot *was kept by the sixteenth-century mystic Rabbi Hayyim Vital of Safed. This student and teacher of Kabbalah [the Jewish mystical tradition] kept a written account of both his dreams and the dreams of others [though it's not clear how their dreams came to him], including them in his* A Book of Visions, *a spiritual autobiography.)*

*I saw in a dream a wealthy man who had died here in Damascus, a year before I came.... He begged me, for God's sake, that I should repair his Soul, because there is nobody else in this generation who is worthy to repair [Souls]. "Tomorrow, I will come to your house so you can repair me." And I awoke.*

*The next day, a girl came to my house.... She was possessed of an evil spirit and I healed her.*

Rabbi Hayyim Vital[1]

- Whom would you like to forgive? Could you give someone who annoyed you the benefit of the doubt?
- Whom would you wish to apologize to for any mistakes you have made? Whom would you like to ask for forgiveness?
- How would you wish God to forgive you?
- Would you like to pray for someone's health or happiness?
- What are your hopes for tomorrow?

Some people choose to write out a *cheshbon hanefesh* over a week's time and then, during the Sabbath, look back at it to get a picture of their lives and to reflect on the movements of their spirit and gauge their progress in turning.

# *Tefilah:* Bedtime Prayers

*Kriyat Sh'ma al hamita,* the recital of the *Sh'ma* at bedtime, is said while you are in bed. Some say it sitting, others say it lying down. Many people only know of one part of the prayer, the familiar *Sh'ma* itself ("Hear O Israel, the Lord our God, the Lord is One"). But as a bedtime prayer, the *Sh'ma* has three central parts. Said regularly and with genuine *kavannah* (spiritual intention or focus), this set of prayers gives us a glimpse of inner peace and prepares us as we journey through the realm of dreams.

## Part I: *Ha'mapil*

The first part is the *Ha'mapil* ("The One who casts") prayer, in which we ask God for a night of good dreams and the secure feeling of protection as we sleep. This prayer for protection at bedtime reflects ancient beliefs that evil spirits could attack one at night.

*Finally we say the Angels' Prayer, which calls upon God to send God's angels to protect us in the night.*

## Ha'mapil

בָּרוּךְ אַתָּה יהוה אֱלֹהֵינוּ מֶלֶךְ הָעוֹלָם,
הַמַּפִּיל חֶבְלֵי שֵׁנָה עַל עֵינָי, וּתְנוּמָה עַל עַפְעַפָּי.
וִיהִי רָצוֹן מִלְּפָנֶיךָ יהוה אֱלֹהַי וֵאלֹהֵי אֲבוֹתַי,
שֶׁתַּשְׁכִּיבֵנִי לְשָׁלוֹם וְתַעֲמִידֵנִי לְשָׁלוֹם.
וְאַל יְבַהֲלוּנִי רַעְיוֹנַי,
וַחֲלוֹמוֹת רָעִים, וְהַרְהוּרִים רָעִים.
וּתְהֵא מִטָּתִי שְׁלֵמָה לְפָנֶיךָ,
וְהָאֵר עֵינַי פֶּן אִישַׁן הַמָּוֶת.
כִּי אַתָּה הַמֵּאִיר לְאִישׁוֹן בַּת עָיִן.
בָּרוּךְ אַתָּה יהוה,
הַמֵּאִיר לָעוֹלָם כֻּלּוֹ בִּכְבוֹדוֹ.

*Baruch Ata, Adonai, Elohenu, Melech ha'olam,*
*Hamapil chevlei sheina al einai*
*u'tenumah al afapai.*
*Vihi ratzon milfanecha, Adonai Elohai v'elohei avotai,*
*shetashkiveni leshalom veta'amideni leshalom.*
*Ve'al yevahaluni rayonai,*
*vacholomot ra'im, veharhorim ra'im.*
*U'tehei mitati sheleima lifanecha,*
*veha'er einai pen ishan hamavet.*
*Ki ata hame'ir le'ishon bat ayin.*
*Baruch Ata, Adonai, hame'ir la'olam kulo bichvodo.*

Blessed are You, our God, gracious One, Keeper of the World,

Who makes my eyes sleepy and causes my eyelids to close.

God of those who came before me,

Help me to lie down peacefully and rise up peacefully.

While I sleep, may I not be disturbed by troubling ideas,

bad dreams, or scary thoughts that come to me in the night.

May my sleep bring both rest and insight.

Blessed are You, God, for illuminating the

whole world in glorious ways.

(adapted translation)


## Part II: *Sh'ma*

The *Sh'ma* is the core statement of Jewish belief and loyalty, essentially the Jewish "Pledge of Allegiance." Even Jews who do not say any other prayers tend to know the *Sh'ma* and admit they say it in times of fear and vulnerability (such as during a turbulent flight) and plan to say it as their last dying words. The deep attachment many have to this prayer may stem from childhood memories of saying this prayer at bedtime with a parent or grandparent and feeling the double-layered protection of both family and God.

When you say this prayer, close your eyes (some cover their eyes with their right hand) so that you can truly hear and feel the words with every inch of your being. As you say the word "hear," focus on the hope that you will hear God's voice in your dreams.

## Sh'ma

שְׁמַ**ע** יִשְׂרָאֵל יהוה אֱלֹהֵינוּ יהוה אֶחָ**ד**.

*Sh'ma Yisra'el Adonai Eloheinu, Adonai echad.*

Hear O Israel, the Lord our God, the Lord is One.

## Part III: Angels' Prayer

Finally we say the Angels' Prayer, which calls upon God to send God's angels to protect us in the night and enable us to feel the security of their presence. Saying this prayer, visualize the protective energies around you that will accompany your dreaming. On your right side is Michael, the angel of love; on your left is Gabriel, the angel of power; before you is Uriel, the angel of light; behind you is Raphael, the angel of healing; and over you is the *Shekhinah,* God's immanent presence. (Both Debbie Friedman and Rabbi Shlomo Carlebach have composed and recorded beautiful lullaby-like melodies for this prayer.)

### The Angel's Prayer

בְּשֵׁם יהוה אֱלֹהֵי יִשְׂרָאֵל,

מִימִינִי מִיכָאֵל, וּמִשְׂמֹאלִי גַּבְרִיאֵל,

וּמִלְּפָנַי אוּרִיאֵל,

וּמֵאֲחוֹרַי רְפָאֵל,

וְעַל רֹאשִׁי שְׁכִינַת אֵל.

*B'shem Adonai, Elohei Yisra'el.*
*mimini Micha'el,*
*u'mismoli Gavriel.*
*u'milfanai Uriel,*
*u'me'achorai Refael,*
*v'al roshi Shekhinat El.*


In the name of the Lord, God of Israel:
May the angel Michael be at my right side,
and at my left side, Gabriel,
before me Uriel,
behind me Raphael,
and above my head, *Shekhinat El,* God's presence.


## Part IV: Holding the *Kavannah* to Dream

As you begin to fall sleep, meditate upon your *kavannah,* your sacred intention, to remember your dreams and to find illumination in them.

*Chalomot paz.* As Israelis wish each other in their version of "sweet dreams": May you have golden dreams.

# chapter four

# Dream Practices for Waking Up

To better recall your dreams, ideally you'd wake up naturally, without an alarm clock. (Granted, this might only be possible when you are on vacation.) As soon as you wake, reach over to your night table and pick up your *sefer chalomot,* your dream book. Lingering in bed, dwell upon any of the dream images or stories that stay in your mind, as if you were remembering a movie. After replaying what you recall, write down as much as you can, keeping the order of your dreams intact if you can, and recording what happened in your dreams in the present tense. Capture all the detail you can recall, even if it doesn't seem especially important to you at the moment, even if it feels trivial or fragmented. Try not to edit out parts of your dreams that are troubling or embarrassing, as you don't want to eliminate any sources of valuable information. The emotional tone of your dreams is very important, so record not only what you saw and heard but also what you felt throughout your dreams.

Some people find it useful to draw their dreams with images rather than with words, so you might also wish to place colored pencils or markers by your bed and use them to illustrate your dreams in your *sefer chalomot*. Include the date and give each dream a distinct title. Finally, ask yourself, "What could this dream be trying to tell me?" and jot down whatever thoughts come into your mind.

If you have a dream in the middle of the night and it wakes you up, you shouldn't risk waiting until morning to write it down. (Keep a flashlight by your bed if the light will distract your partner.)

Make keeping your *sefer chalomot* a priority, and you will be rewarded, for doing so stimulates more regular dream recall. These questions may help jog your memory:

- Who was in the dream?
- What were people wearing?
- What did they say?
- What color were objects that surrounded you?
- What was the landscape like?
- If people you know were in your dream, how were they like or unlike their real-life versions?

It's worth noting that there are distinctions between the actual dream you had, the dream you recall, and the written narrative you construct in your *sefer chalomot*. Your memory of your dream and your written reconstruction of it are both at a distance from the actual dream and reflect creative choices you make as you possess the dream for yourself. Consequently, just by remembering and writing down your dream, you are already beginning to interpret it.

# Expressing Gratitude in the Morning

Having recorded your dreams, you are finally ready to greet the day. Sleep, the sages teach us, is one-sixtieth of death, meaning that even though it is a time of higher consciousness, the powerlessness and inactivity we experience in sleep give us a taste of death that can feel disconcerting. Awake and fully conscious in the morning, we are relieved to discover that we are re-created as persons who have the power to operate our limbs, our lips, our minds, and our hearts in loving and productive ways. This is a cause for celebration! Rising, we can also express gratitude for our good night's sleep, for the richness of our dreams, and for the capacity to remember them by reciting a version of the blessing for waking up, the *Modeh Ani* prayer.

### *Modeh Ani*

מוֹדֶה אֲנִי לְפָנֶיךָ, מֶלֶךְ חַי וְקַיָּם.

מוֹדָה אֲנִי לְפָנֶיךָ, מֶלֶךְ חַי וְקַיָּם.

*Modeh ani l'fanekha* (for a male)

*Modah ani l'fanekha* (for a female)

Thank you, God, for waking me up and giving me this new day.

(adapted translation)

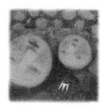

# chapter five

# Practices for Interpreting Dreams

*A dream, self-interpreted: Once again, I (Vanessa) have my recurring dream. I am living in a house and, while walking through, discover there is an entire wing I have not even noticed before. I open a door and enter a rustic wood bedroom and start opening dresser drawers and pulling out scarves, a kimono, jewelry, and mementos that belonged to the person who lived there before. It's all mine now, and it's all wonderful, and I'm happy to have it. The whole time I'm going through the booty I chastise myself, "How could you have been so unobservant, to have lived here this long and never looked beyond the closed door, never even questioned what was on the other side?" Here's where the dream always becomes a lucid dream, because I find myself*

Whether you believe that dreams are messages from God or from deep places inside our souls or imaginations, you know they have something to teach. For dreams are not just curious stories of the night. They are hopes, wishes, insights, and sources of profound information that are too important to ignore.

## Seeking Interpretation

With dreams now inscribed in your *sefer chalomot,* you will want to make sense of them, for as the Rabbis taught, the meaning of a dream becomes clear only when it is interpreted. Jewish textual culture is, at its core, interpretive: it is not thinkable to read Scripture or Talmud and say, "This is literally what it means." One is always digging deeply under the surface, interpreting the texts in dialogue with generations of commentators.

## Interpreting Dreams as Your Own

You can try to interpret your dreams on your own. If you are uncomfortable bringing your dreams to others for interpretation, you can still use the same techniques and instructions (see below) for interpreting your own dreams. You may find that if you write down your thoughts (as opposed to just thinking them through), you will discover a wider range of possible interpretations. Keep in mind the basic tenet of Jewish dream interpretation: every dream, even a seemingly horrific one, presents us with the potential to transform it into something good.

## Seeking a Dream Interpreter

Alternatively, you can seek out help in interpretation. Many cultures have oneiromancers, spiritual guides who help individuals think through their dreams and who can unlock their hidden meanings, and Judaism is no exception. From biblical and Talmudic texts, we get the sense that in antiquity both strategies—self-interpretation and interpretation with assistance—were used. The dreamer probably consulted an expert in dream interpretation only for dreams so enigmatic or so disturbing that they couldn't be resolved on one's own. Dreams that recurred or came at a critical juncture in one's life, such as before a trip or before making a major decision, were probably the ones that called out for professional attention.

The wise person you turn to could be a rabbi, teacher, spiritual advisor, or therapist. The person need not be specially trained in dream interpretation but must value dreams and consider them important. It could be a wise family member or friend; someone who knows you fairly well and makes you feel

being somewhat aware that I am dreaming. I recall that I have had similar dreams before, only to wake up disappointed to find that my own house has no secret chambers. But then I always decide: "No, this is not a dream; this is the real thing. All the other dreams were a premonition that prepared me for today!"

I jump out of bed when I wake up, ready to start washing, ironing, and putting away the things I have found. When I discover it is once again a dream, I am disappointed and feel a little stupid, as if a practical joke had been played on me.

When I try to interpret this dream, I decide it links my soul to a teaching of the Hasidic master the Baal Shem Tov, who taught that each day holds at least one hundred opportunities to express gratitude for what we have. How little we need to wish for when the most valuable treasures we have are already ours: the qualities of our character, the gift of our body, the many people we're connected to, and the bounty of things that sustains us and gives us joy. My dream puts me in touch with a primary spiritual goal: to be vigilant about noticing my blessings and expressing my gratitude for them.

(Author David Mamet has had this recurring dream as long as he can remember. It keeps him adhering to his core commitment to be a writer who is a vigilant social critic.)

In the dream I have killed someone. I tell myself, in the dream, that I have had this dream before, that the murder is not real, that it is, again, just a dream. Then a sense of reality overcomes me, and I know past certainty that this time the dream is real, that I have killed, and all the world is against me.

(Mamet explains that the meaning he makes of this dream, called a lucid dream because one is aware that one is dreaming, concerns the persona he needs to maintain as a writer. Mamet's dream reminds him that he needs to hold on to his identity as an iconoclast, even when society rewards him with success.)

This must mean not subscribing to the social contract but resisting it—saying or being prepared to say the unacceptable.

David Mamet[1]

safe; someone whose intuition and insights you trust; someone whose concern is to help and not to judge. (Persons to avoid: those who try to convince you that they can see through your dreams to your repressed wishes and childhood traumas, and those who take a prurient interest in dreams of a sexual nature.) Select a person who has the ability to read you like a book, someone who is so sensitive to your feelings that he or she knows them even before you say a word.

Alternatively, you might seek out or choose to create a group of like-minded souls in your community to meet regularly, perhaps with a trained facilitator, to work on dream interpretations together.

You might find many wise dream interpreters in your life, and each one may offer a different and equally wise interpretation. Rabbi Bana'ah once taught, "There were twenty-four dream interpreters who lived in Jerusalem. Once, I had a dream and went to *each* of the twenty-four dream interpreters to ask them to interpret my dream. Not a single one interpreted the dream in the same way: I had twenty-four different interpretations! Yet every interpretation was correct!" Thus, the Rabbi concluded, "All dreams follow the mouth (Babylonian Talmud, *Brakhot* 55b)," meaning that there is no single correct interpretation of a dream but rather multiple possible interpretations that could each reveal some true and important aspect of its meaning.

How can you know if the dream interpretation you have received is correct for you? Some say you will experience a tingle, an "Aha!" of recognition, which comes as a sign that you are being connected to a deep truth. Remember: no matter how pious, wise, or well credentialed your interpreter is, you are the only one who knows whether an interpretation provides illumination or direction for you.

# Guidelines for Being a Dream Interpreter

You may be the person to whom others come for help when their dreams need interpretation. These guidelines, based on both secular and Jewish wisdom, can help you fine-tune the innate skills in dream interpretation that others may believe you have.

- Listen deeply to the entire dream before rushing to interpret it. Dream interpretation isn't an exact science, and you are certainly not expected to come up with the "correct" interpretation. It may turn out that the best gift you can give as an interpreter isn't your interpretation but your willingness to listen in a focused way.

- Listen to the language of the dream, as there are often clues in how people word their dream narratives. For instance, a dreamer who explains, "I was in the car, but I wasn't in the driver's seat," may be expressing feelings of being out of control.

- Feel free to ask why the dreamer thinks the dream may have come and how it may be tied to what's going on in his or her waking life.

- Pay attention to the questions that grab you as you listen to the dream. What associations does the dreamer have with the specific images in the dream? What feelings does the dream evoke? Ideally, you will try to elicit an interpretation from the dreamer, who knows what's happening best of all.

- Know in advance that not all parts of a dream will make sense. As the Talmud teaches, "There is no dream without elements of nonsense." The sages taught that when

*Woke up in the middle of the night. And suddenly remembered my important dream. A few minutes of intense effort to bring it back…had the feeling that the dream was part of my personality, that I had the right to hang on to it, that I must not let it escape me, that I had to be certain of it if I am to be a rounded and whole person…*

*My sudden eating complex elicited a dream last night. It was very clear, at least I thought so, but now that I want to write it all down much of it has gone. A lot of people round a table with S. at the head. He said something like, "Why don't you go and visit other people?" And I, "Because of all that bother about eating." And then he gave me that famous look of his that I would need a whole lifetime to put on paper…and I read in it something like, "So that's what you're really like, eating is all that matters to you." And I suddenly got a feeling of, "He's seen right through me…" I haven't described this dream properly, it cannot be done. However, what can be described is the sudden realization: now he has seen through me, knows what I am really like. And the horror of it.*

Etty Hillesum[2]

*One should not tell a dream save to a friend.*

(*Zohar* II:182b)

*When one has had a dream, one should unburden oneself of it before friends so that they should express their good wishes and utter words of good omen.*

(*Zohar* II:200a)

wheat is ground to make flour, inevitably some straw sneaks into the final product by mistake. So too, whenever a person dreams, inevitably some degree of nonsense sneaks in. You should therefore feel free to address the parts of a dream that seem most meaningful.

• Choose the most favorable way to interpret the dream. Every dream—even a violent, disturbing one—holds within it the possibility of a positive interpretation. The sages tell the story of a man who once dreamt that both of his legs would fall off. The rabbi interpreting his dream said, "This dream signifies that you will become so rich that you will have the luxury of riding everywhere on horseback, rather than walking on foot." If you see a choice between interpreting a dream in a positive or a negative light, pick the positive interpretation.

# chapter six

# Practices for Dream Incubation

Many wisdom traditions have a practice of dream incubation, in which one performs rituals before going to sleep in order to connect to the Divine and to pose a specific question. In some cultures, the dreamer went to an ancient temple or holy site, made sacrifices, and actually slept there, hoping to receive dreams that would provide insights, answers, comfort, or healing. There were probably ritual experts skilled in dream interpretation who made their services available at the sites.

This ancient practice of dream incubation, which Jews refer to as *she'elat chalom,* "asking a dream question," has been carried out since the days of the Bible and has continued in later Jewish mystical practices until this day.

You, too, can incubate a dream when you have a special concern or problem that is on your mind, something bothering or troubling you, or an issue you can't consciously solve in the daytime no matter how hard you concentrate. You can intend to receive a dream, a divine message, which gives you strength and vision or the solution to a problem, whether it is personal, intellectual, creative, or spiritual. The dream you receive may not provide an obvious or overt answer to your question, but it may still illuminate your path as you decide what to do, or it may provide you with insights into your personality.

The notion of dream incubation may seem strange to you, but you have probably had the experience many times without consciously giving it a name. Consider all the times you have gone to sleep with an unresolved issue and then woken up in the morning simply knowing what to do. This is the experience of countless writers, painters, musicians, scientists, engineers, inventors, and administrators who have spent the day consciously trying—and failing—to resolve issues, only to wake up from their dreams with creative solutions in mind (hence, the expression "Sleep on it"). Some can trace the solution directly to a dream; for others, it is a subliminal clarity or clue that comes their way.

Before learning how you can engage in the practice of *she'elat chalom,* you may wish to study some traditional Jewish models of dream incubation drawn from the Bible. Hagar, Jacob, and King Solomon were all dream incubators who prepared for their dreams by asking for insight, inspiration, and wisdom. Jewish mystics later took them as models as they adapted the practice of *she'elat chalom* for themselves. We can be similarly inspired, knowing that we come from a long line of dream incubators.

*In her dream, Hagar learned self-sufficiency. Her dream*
*inspired clarity of vision and action and conspired*
*against despair: wipe away your tears; open your eyes.*

# Hagar (Genesis 21:14–21)

Some biblical scholars believe that Hagar was a dream incubator who went to a special place, Be'ersheva, where she encountered God in her dream and received help (admittedly, this requires some reading between the lines).

Hagar, the Egyptian maidservant of the matriarch Sarah, had been cast out, along with Ishmael, the son she had with Abraham, into the wilderness. Hagar and her son wandered until they had no water left and would surely die. Hagar engaged in the practice of dream incubation when, reaching Be'ersheva, she placed her son under a bush and sat herself down a distance away. She appealed to God to witness her dire situation and offer help in the form of a dream communication. It is possible to understand the tears she shed as a heartfelt, eloquent prayer. Then Hagar fell asleep.

God's voice was carried from heaven by an angel who called to Hagar in her dream, asking her what the matter was. The angel advised her not to be fearful, for God was in touch with the suffering of her son and felt his pain. In the dream, Hagar was told to embrace her boy, hold him by the hand, and believe that one day, no matter how bleak things were just now, he would be the father of a great nation. When Hagar awoke, she saw a well of water (*be'er,* the site's namesake, means "well"). Perhaps the well was actually there before her dream, but Hagar could not yet see it. This is a frequent gift of a dream or a waking insight: the ability to see what was there in front of us all along. Hagar filled her skin with water, let her son drink, and he was revived. We might imagine that after Hagar revived her son, she took care of herself, understanding that a caring parent must take good care of herself. It is possible that she learned self-care in her dream as well.

In her dream, Hagar learned self-sufficiency. Her dream inspired clarity of vision and action and conspired against despair: wipe away your tears; open your eyes. Her dream gave her the psychic strength to become the mother of a new nation. Hagar was the first person to forge a new society without the protection of a spouse, a tribe, or a community.

## Jacob (Genesis 28:10–22)

Jacob, sent off by his parents to Haran to look for a wife, was all alone. We can imagine that he was scared and worried. Would he succeed in his quest? Would he survive his journey all by himself? With these questions in mind, Jacob prepared to incubate a dream. He selected a particular stone that he found in the place that he would eventually call Beth-El: the house of God. Something about the stone and the place itself must have struck him as having the potential for a divine encounter. He used the chosen stone as his pillow. He had a dream, a vision of angels going up and down a ladder between earth and heaven. He heard the voice of God, who promised he would indeed be blessed with all good things and safety. Jacob awoke from his dream relieved. He knew God had been in that place with him even while he was asleep. He transformed the stone that had been his pillow into a shrine by pouring oil on it so that others might come there, too, and experience their own connection to God. Then he vowed that if God really did come through for him, as promised in his dream, he would pledge to God a tenth of all his wealth to express his gratitude.

## King Solomon (I Kings 3)

As a young man, King Solomon didn't feel up to the task of ruling a nation, particularly when he compared himself to his father, the accomplished King David. He turned to God for help, going to Gibeon to incubate a dream. Before going to sleep, King Solomon prepared himself spiritually to hear the voice of God in his dreams by offering a thousand sacrifices, a demonstrative gesture, part prayer and part emergency flare. Solomon slept close to the altar. The embers still burned, and perhaps he could smell the many burnt offerings that had been made. These were not just his sacrifices alone but were also those of others who, like King Solomon, had come hoping to encounter God in *their* dreams so that God could answer their questions and strengthen them to face their own anxieties. Solomon had his request for God ready in his mind: "What wisdom can you give me to help me do my job with confidence and success?"

In his dream, Solomon heard God encouraging him to speak his mind. Solomon asked for a wise heart. Impressed by Solomon's modest and selfless request, God not only promised Solomon the wise and understanding heart he asked for, but wealth and fame as well.

Solomon awoke from his dream. He must have experienced tremendous assurance from this dream. In gratitude for this reassuring dream, Solomon immediately went to Jerusalem and expressed his thanks to God by offering even more sacrifices and by making a feast.

Solomon's request for a wise heart might remind us of the character in the *Wizard of Oz,* the Tin Man, who went with Dorothy to the Wizard requesting a heart. The Tin Man, through his compassionate actions, demonstrated that he certainly had a heart—only he didn't know it. The same was so for King Solomon: he already had a wise heart. He needed the confidence to trust that his God-given heart was sufficiently wise. Solomon learned in his incubated dream what we ourselves might learn: that we already have abundant gifts and sufficient talent to do the tasks required of us.

## Asking Your Own *She'elat Chalom*

You will want to prepare thoroughly to incubate your dream. As Joel Covitz has written, "If the dream is a manifestation of the Divine, then the bedtime incantation or prayer sets the stage for the epiphany."[1] Jewish tradition holds many "recipes" for how to carry out the Jewish dream incubation ritual. Think of it as a kind of prayer, not one uttered hastily or mindlessly, but one that requires intense readiness and presence.

You will need to prepare both yourself and your room for the *she'elat chalom* ritual. (You will also want to let anyone who shares a bedroom with you know what you're up to and ask for support.) These activities can put you into a trancelike state allowing you to experience heightened intuition. People once fasted on the day of their dream incubation. You might choose to spend the day eating lightly, perhaps by having a liquid diet; by taking small meals of fruits, vegetables, and whole grains; or by avoiding wine or meat. During the day, engage in some form of a purification ritual. This could mean going to a *mikvah*, a Jewish ritual bath, if one is available in your community. Alternatively, you could immerse yourself in a lake or ocean with thoughts of spiritual purification, or take a long calming bath with the express intention of becoming ready to enter into communication with the Divine. More simply, you might just wash your hands or put freshly laundered sheets on your bed as a symbol of spiritual cleansing and readiness.

Prepare your bedroom for the incubation by making it especially clean. If your concerns are about a particular person, select a photograph of that person and place it nearby. Or choose a cherished object that gives you strength, solace, or a

*Rabbi Hayyim Vital was a frequent incubator of dreams.*

1563: On the first night of Cheshvan (a Jewish month in the fall) I asked a dream question, about a certain woman, whether she was my predestined mate....

1565: My wife, Hannah, was engaged to me and we had a dispute. I asked a dream question, as to whether I should marry her.... I was answered with a verse: Go say to them, "Return to your tents" (Deuteronomy 5:27).[2]

connection to your ancestors. I know that when my mother has special worries she wants to meditate upon, she takes out items that she inherited from her parents—her father's yarmulke and prayer book, her mother's Sabbath scarf—and place them nearby. Through the placement of these objects, she signals to her ancestors that she needs their help in bringing her prayers before God.

Before bedtime, spend about 20 minutes writing in a journal, focusing on the specific problem you wish to resolve with the aid of dreaming. Speculate on the cause of your problem, think about solutions that might work, and consider what you have to gain and lose by solving your problem now. Note how reflecting upon your problem makes you feel right now.

Before you go to sleep, write down your question as a one-line sentence that you also hold in your mind. You might even place that sentence under your pillow.

As an alternative to journal writing, you could lie in bed and, once you have fully relaxed, muscle by muscle, meditate upon the question that concerns you. In that relaxed state, bring your concerns before God and request insights through the dreams that will come to you. Express your intention to recall the divine communications that may come to you and your desire to discern God's voice in your dreams.

Then, based on a practice of the kabbalist Rabbi Hayyim Vital, just before you go to sleep, say:

> *May it be your will, God of our mothers and fathers,*
> *May this question I have in my dreams be answered.*

Or you might prefer this petition:

> *"Master of Dreams, before I {state your name} enter your*
> *world of healing and visions, I place myself at your*

*(Other dream incubation techniques practiced by Jews of old include visiting a cemetery and weeping copious tears. A story is told in the Midrash:)*

*A student of Rabbi Simeon bar Yohai had forgotten what he learned. In tears, he went to the cemetery. Because he wept so, his teacher Rabbi Simeon came to him in a dream and told him, "When you wail, throw three bundles and I shall come." The student went to a dream interpreter and told him what happened. The interpreter instructed, "Repeat the chapter you are learning three times and you will then remember it." The student did just that, and it worked.*

(Midrash Rabbah
Kohelet 10:10)

*disposal. I am facing the following concerns and issues*
*that are in need of your guidance…*
*I beseech You—the fountain of wisdom, insight, and*
*healing—to help me find my path…."*[3]

Whenever you wake up—even if it's in the middle of the night—write down in your *sefer chalomot,* your dream book, the details of the dream you incubated. Remember that sometimes the dream-answer doesn't come right away. You may need to repeat your dream question for several nights before you receive the dream that speaks to you.

Once you have received a dream, use it to work toward clarifying your problem by interpreting it. This work requires that you trust your intuition to discover the guidance your dream offers. Don't look for literal solutions to your dream question: they may come as images that spark off a set of associations. Pay attention to all potential symbols in your dream, both the central images and the ones that appear in the periphery. What associations and feelings do they evoke for you? After you note what literal situations in your life the dream may be alluding to, look for coded clues. For instance, if your dream question was, "Is this the right time to break up with my partner?" and in your dream you recall the closing of a door or the cutting of a ribbon, you may have an answer that it is indeed time to seek closure or sever ties.

You might choose to bring your dream to a friend, family member, therapist, or spiritual teacher to gain the wisdom of their insights. We have blind spots and might miss clues that our incubated dreams are sending us. But remember: although others can make suggestions about the meaning of your dreams, only you can know whether the dream you have incubated provides a workable solution.

# chapter seven

# Practices for Responding to Nightmares: *Hatavat Chalom*

## (Transforming a Bad Dream into a Good One)

It is particularly important to pay attention to our troubling dreams. The very fact that they disturb us is an indication that they hold within them urgent messages, which can be understood as coming from the unconscious or a divine source telling us, "Attention must be paid." It has been suggested that there really is no such thing as a "bad dream." All dreams come in the service of health and wholeness and can be interpreted in constructive ways.

Despite the positive potential of nightmares, they can still feel awful. As Rabbi Chisda taught in the Talmud, "Seeing a negative dream is worse than receiving a lashing." You might suspect that only a terrible person would have such a terrible dream. The Talmud offers consolation: even the celebrated King David had frequent nightmares; in fact, he never had a positive dream. The Talmud records several practices to help people who have had bad dreams and wish to make them better—that is, to make sense of them and relieve any lingering feelings of fear or foreboding so that they can go about their day without feeling terrified and out of kilter.

In the first practice, you hold a dream court, gathering three friends who will come help you with your dream. In the second set of practices, which take place in synagogue when you are praying with others, you keep your troubling dream private but deal with it in a communal setting. The third set of practices can be done all by yourself. A fourth practice, contemporary in origin, encourages you not to let go of the nightmare, but to hold onto it. The variety of practices acknowledges that each of us has different levels of comfort when it comes to revealing our dreams or bringing others into conversation about our dream lives.

# Dream Court

If you have a nightmare that has upset you, gather three friends (or family members who are like friends) who will help you confront your troubling dream by performing the ritual of *hatavat chalom,* "making a dream better." Your friends will compose what was once called a dream court. They should be trusted friends, friends who know you well. Ideally, they should be friends who will not tease you for taking a troubling dream so seriously. Explain to your friends that you are asking their help in performing an ancient Talmudic ritual that will help you find positive meanings in a troubling dream. Assure them that the ceremony is brief and not in the least bit

*If you have a nightmare that has upset you, gather three friends who will help you confront your troubling dream by performing the ritual of* hatavat chalom, *"making a dream better."*

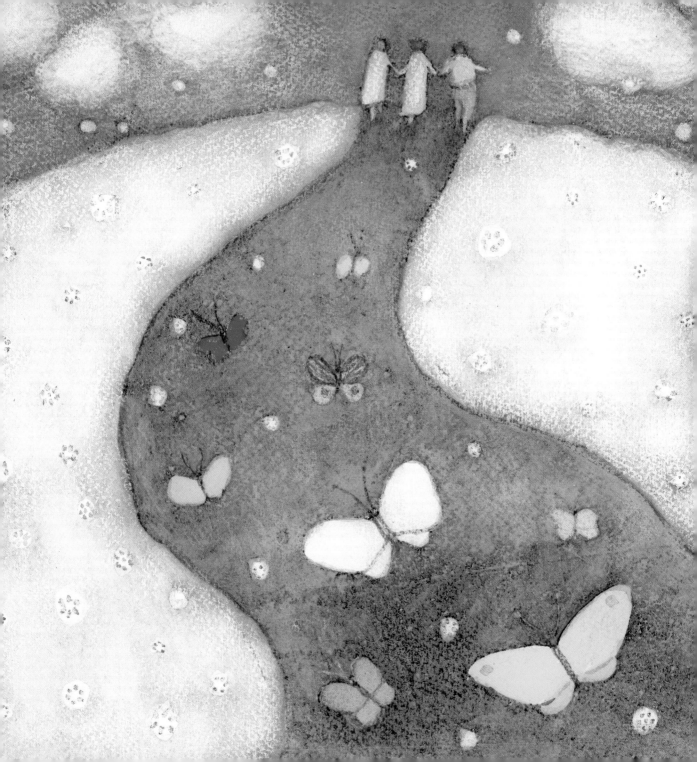

strange. Let them know whether this is a new ritual for you and that you may need their good will and forbearance. Ask them to keep what they hear confidential.

You can decide *not* to let them know the precise contents of your dream, and they can still help you turn your bad dream into a good one. If you *do* feel comfortable letting your friends know what you dreamt and are willing to share why it was so troubling, they might be able to help you find its meaning and provide support as you discover how it can connect with the rest of your life. They might be able to show you how your bad dream really was a good dream in disguise.

Tell them:

*"I have seen a good dream." (Here, you can decide whether or not to tell them anything about what was, in fact, your* bad *dream.)*

They should say to you:

*"It is a good dream! May God transform it so it will be better." (They are clearly using the power of positive thinking.)*

Then, all together, your friends should say these three traditional verses from the Torah about transformation from sorrow to joy:

*"You turn my mourning into dancing";*

*"You turn their mourning into joy";*

*"You turn curses into blessings."*

They should then say three verses from the Torah about redemption:

*"God has rescued my soul";*

*"Those God rescues will return singing";*

*"And the people rescued Jonathan."*

Then they should recite three verses from the Torah about peace:

*"Peace, peace, to those far and near";*

*"Peace, peace, to you and to all who help you";*

*"Peace, peace, unto you, peace unto your house, and peace on all that you have."*

Together you can say:

*"May God turn all our dreams to good ones, and may we help to make our good dreams come true."*

In lieu of reciting these traditional verses, your friends could instead share their own stories about times when bad things happened that turned out to be not so bad after all because they were opportunities for growth, self-discovery, or mastery of skills. Elicit such stories by requesting them to:

1. Tell you about something sad that happened that eventually was transformed into a source of joy.
2. Tell you about an experience that started out bad, but somehow got redeemed.

## Hatavat Chalom *in Literature*

*(In S. Ansky's play,* The Dybbuk, *Rabbi Samson has a bad dream and convenes a dream court:)*

*RABBI AZRAEL, MICHOEL AND THE TWO JUDGES: You beheld a good dream! You beheld a good dream! You beheld a good dream!*

*RABBI AZRAEL: We have found a solution of good to your dream.*

*RABBI SAMSON: I beheld a good dream—a good dream I beheld. I beheld a good dream.*

S. Ansky[1]

3. Tell you about an experience of strife, struggle, or disagreement that eventually led to peace and harmony.

If you have shared your dream and your friends have interpretations to share with you, hear them out. Thank them by promising to be there for them if they should ever need you when they have a troubling dream.

# Synagogue Practices

If you have had an upsetting dream, you can address the troubling feeling the dream has left you with when you are in synagogue. The advantage of this practice is that you have both the experience of community and privacy for, while you are not alone, no one needs to know that you have had a nightmare or that you are performing a *hatavat chalom*.

The ritual is based on a very old one that is still performed in some Orthodox synagogues on the major festivals (Sukkot, Passover, and Shavuot) during the priestly blessing of the *musaf*, or additional service. The descendents of the Temple priests, the *kohanim*, offer a blessing during the silent *amidah* prayer called *birkat kohanim* (priestly blessing) for all the members of the congregation. It's a wonderfully eerie and holy experience if you've ever seen it performed. The *kohanim* wash their hands, take off their shoes, cover their heads with their *tallitot* (prayer shawls), hold their hands up in a gesture of blessing, and sing an incantation. Some people have a tradition of not looking at the *kohanim* as they say their blessing (although my grandmother told me I'd go blind if I looked, I always peeked, and still do, I confess). While the *kohanim* are saying their blessing, the congregants, on their own, quietly recite to themselves a *hatavat chalom* prayer, like the one you see below. It is said both by people who have had troubling

*(Ellen Frankel, in her contemporary feminist biblical commentary, The Five Books of Miriam, explores the ritual of* hatavat chalom *from two angles, one accepting of the old practices and one cynical.)*

*Dinah the Wounded One cries: You think Pharaoh has disturbing dreams? We should all be so lucky! What nightmares haunt my dreams!*

*The Rabbis counsel: If you have bad dreams, it is a good idea to fast and repent. If the dream is very disturbing, you may even fast on the Sabbath or a festival day. You should gather together three good friends and perform the following ritual:*

*The three friends should face the dreamer and recite together: Do not interpretations belong to God? Relate it to me, if you please.*

*Then the dreamer says, seven times: I have seen a good dream.*

*The friends repeat: You have seen a good dream. It is good and may it become good. May the Merciful One transform it to the good. May it be decreed seven times from heaven that it become good and always be good. It is good and may it become good.*

*Dinah responds: If only it were so simple!*

Ellen Frankel[2]

## Interpreting Your Bad Dreams

*A nightmare: I (Elizabeth) had been working at a coffee shop all summer, and last night I had my first coffee shop nightmare. Mobs of angry and rude customers wanted their espressos and cappuccinos but there was no coffee left, not even a bean. What's more, no one was paying for anything and everyone was sneering at me.*

*In the fleeting moments just after I woke up, my dream still felt so blaringly real. In my dream I was powerless; I had to accept my fate. I could not take the problem into my own hands, brew some more coffee, and address my customers' pressing need for caffeine fixes. There was no coffee, and I could only suffer the repercussions.*

*When I was more awake, I talked the dream through with my mother. By then, I could reflect on my anxiety-ridden dream and even laugh about it. I was able to ask myself, "What is the big deal?"*

dreams of their own and by people who are concerned about having appeared in the troubling dreams of others. In both cases, the prayer expresses the hope that the upsetting dream will be transformed into a good one.

If this practice of the priestly blessing is performed in your synagogue, while it is going on, you can silently offer a prayer expressing your desire that you will discover a way to find a positive interpretation for your dream. Alternatively, you can offer this prayer when your rabbi offers a blessing for the entire congregation. Sometimes this blessing will come at the very end of the service, when all rise as the rabbi offers a version of the priestly blessing, which usually begins, "May the Lord bless you and keep you...."

If your synagogue practices neither a *birkat kohanim* nor a rabbi's blessing, you can still quietly and privately say the *hatavat chalom* prayer to yourself at any point in the service. When you hear your fellow congregants saying "Amen" (meaning, Let it be so!) to any prayer at all, consider the "Amen" as a sign that you are supported by your community as you seek to find positive meaning in your dream. Although you're not divulging your troubling dream to a soul, and certainly not to the entire congregation, you can still imaginatively experience their supportive presence at this time.

The *hatavat chalom* prayer you can say in synagogue is:

*Source of the Universe,*
*I am yours and my dreams are yours.*
*I have had a dream, but I don't know what it means.*
*May it be your will, God of our mothers and fathers:*
*If my dream requires healing, may You strengthen, heal, and transform my dream.*

*Just as You have transformed curses into blessings,*
*Please transform all of my dreams concerning myself*
*or others into good ones.*
*May You protect me, show kindness to me, and accept me.*
*Amen.*

# Private Practices

There are two Jewish practices you can engage in when you are disturbed by a bad dream and you neither feel comfortable about revealing it to anyone nor wish to focus on it while in the presence of your praying community. One ancient practice recorded in the Talmudic period is called a *ta'anit chalom*, a "dream fast." Apparently people could be so disturbed by a bad dream that the rabbis permitted them to fast and pray that their bad dream be turned into a good one even when it occurred on the Sabbath, a time when fasting (with the exception of Yom Kippur falling on the Sabbath) would be otherwise forbidden.

A second, more contemporary practice can be useful when a bad dream wakes you up in the middle of the night and no one is around. The practice is attributed to Samuel, one of the Talmudic sages, who, when he had a bad dream, found comfort by meditating alone upon this brief verse from the Book of Zechariah (10:2): "Dreams speak lies." In other words, in his meditational practice, Samuel affirmed that he had the power to decide if a dream was going to trouble him or illuminate him. Following Samuel's practice, if you have a disturbing dream and you have decided holding on to the dream will cause you more pain than good, in your own private meditation you can remind yourself that only you have the power to determine the meaning of your dreams.

*This dream prompted me to recite a private prayer, because I was grateful that I have the ability to recognize what is "real" and what is "unreal." I was thankful that I could separate myself from the anxiety-ridden parts of my dream and tear off the layers of tension from my body that had formed during my dreaming. This way, my dream did not gnaw at me. Rather, once awake, I regained my power to recognize distinctions between my dream life and my waking life and was able to begin my day anew.*

*My own private prayer was inspired by the traditional Jewish morning prayers in which we say: Praised are You, Lord our God, Ruler of the Universe, who enables your creatures to distinguish between night and day.*

*Literally, this prayer is about our being grateful that there are roosters who know when it's time to wake us up with their cock-a-doodle-doo. Figuratively, it's about our ability to know when it's time to get up and to have the energy to greet the day. It helped me mark a separation between the images of my distressing night vision and the image of a fresh new day. It helped me to be*

If a bad dream wakes you in the night and sleep eludes you, turn to your *sefer chalomot* and let writing down your dream and writing about the feelings it raises help restore your composure.

You might recite these comforting words from the familiar *Adon Olam* prayer:

*I place my spirit in God's care,*
*When I wake as when I sleep.*
*God is with me, with my body and spirit:*
*I shall not fear.*

## Holding on to a Nightmare

Although people often want to do something to make the discomfort of a nightmare go away, you may feel at times there is a reason to stay with disturbing dreams, even if they keep returning night after night. Some disturbing dreams are worth holding on to for the illumination they might reveal. Instead of transforming a particular nightmare, you decide to let it transform you as you wait for it to reveal its teachings over time. This can be compared to the way that Jews do not forget the past, but retell the stories of tragedies and traumas as a way of remembering them each year, in order to be sensitized and instructed by history. In remembering, there can be healing.

Dr. Rachel Naomi Remen, author of *Kitchen Table Wisdom*, describes a time when she made the choice to hold on to a particular group of nightmares. When Dr. Remen was working as a pediatrician and was learning how to encounter death as a source of healing, she had a series of disturbing dreams. She would find herself at the bedside of pediatric

*grateful for the power I have to take control of my life.*

*Another nightmare: This was a horrible dream! I was standing alone in the middle of a farm. A dead chicken lay just in front of my feet. I knew in my dream that if I took one more step past the decapitated chicken, I would see a formerly close friend lying dead in the field. Luckily, I woke up before this gruesome and upsetting image could fully surface in my mind.*

*That morning, after talking through the dream with my mother, I called my old friend, whom I had not spoken with in quite some time. She had figuratively been "dead" in my life. It felt easy to reconnect and our relationship was repaired and got back on course.*

*To be honest, I do not believe an all-powerful deity was sending me a prophetic message about this particular friendship in my dream. But I do believe that by listening to my dream about the dead chicken, I was led to reconnect with my friend.*

patients who had died long ago. Although she had forgotten the details of their cases, she recalled in vivid dreams every last detail of their lives: their lab reports, their conversations, even their stuffed animals. She recalled, "the most frightening part of these dreams was that eventually…I would come to feel what I had not allowed myself to feel, feelings of sadness, pain, helplessness and loss." She would wake up nightly crying after these dreams and asked a psychiatrist friend for advice. He advised her to stay with the dreams until she saw what they meant, and he offered to hear them out. This went on for many days, until she no longer saw the children's deaths "as a personal failure but as universal mystery." Enduring these dreams ended up preparing her for her life's work with people facing difficult illnesses, teaching her more than she could have ever learned from any book.[3]

If you choose to endure a stretch of nightmares without engaging in some ritual of transformation, you would be advised to get professional counsel and support in the process, just as Dr. Remen did.

chapter eight

# Holding a Rosh Chodesh Gathering Devoted to Dreaming

In the last two decades, Jewish women have been gathering on the night of the New Moon, called *Rosh Chodesh*. Rosh Chodesh is an ancient Jewish women's holiday that has been re-created as a monthly occasion for women to come together, usually in informal home settings, to study, pray, and celebrate their Jewish and female identities. Rosh Chodesh marks the beginning of each month of the Jewish calendar, which is lunar, not solar. (Jewish bookstores and Jewish holiday websites have Jewish calendars that indicate when each new Jewish month starts.)

*The New Moon is taken as an occasion to dwell on the illumination that dreams and their interpretation can bring into one's life.*

The theme of dreams would be an important topic for any month's Rosh Chodesh gathering. Clearly, Jewish women have been both dreamers and dream interpreters, but without much written record, we have not been able to tell their stories, honor them, or see them as mentors. What's more, the moon has long been a symbol of illumination, so it's fitting that the beginning of a New Moon is taken as an occasion to dwell on the illumination that dreams and their interpretation can bring into one's life.

Convene your regular Rosh Chodesh group or take the opportunity to start one, inviting about ten women friends to join you at sunset, either on the eve of a New Moon or on a Sunday evening (a time many have free) nearest to the New Moon. The women needn't all know each other or even be of the same age group, but they should be people who will respect and support each other, listen with sensitivity, and honor the confidentiality of what transpires when you meet. You might want to invite some women who have had experience working with dreams in a group setting. Meet in a home or private setting, indoors or out. If your meeting is indoors, set the mood with candles and soft music. Serve hot drinks for the cold months or cool drinks for summer evenings. Some serve sweets as omens of a sweet new month; some serve cookies and fruits cut into crescent shapes.

Below is a plan for a Rosh Chodesh gathering devoted to dreams. Recently, groups of Jewish girls, usually sixth and seventh graders, have started meeting on Rosh Chodesh (usually with an adult group leader), so we provide additional suggestions for a girls' gathering.

## Welcome

Introduce yourselves. Welcome each other and celebrate your being together by singing:

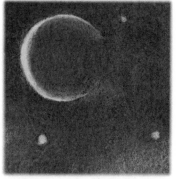

*Speaking to young people, in particular, about sharing dreams:*

*Even if you hesitate to share your dreams, you still might want to push yourself to share one with a close friend who is willing to explore your dream with you.*

*After dreaming, we often feel bewildered and alone. As many of us prefer to control every aspect of our daily lives, it is often difficult to admit that elements of our dreams have entered our minds without our consent. Our reactions to dreams often exhibit our embarrassment or shock: "I can't believe I dreamed of kissing him!" "Why was I still obsessing about what she said? I thought I was over it!"*

הִנֵּה מַה־טּוֹב וּמַה־נָּעִים שֶׁבֶת נָשִׁים גַּם־יָחַד.

*Hineh mah tov u'ma'naim, shevet nashim gam yachad.*

How good and how pleasant it is when women gather together.

Welcome the New Moon and introduce the theme of dreaming by lighting a candle in honor of Rosh Chodesh and saying:

> Blessed are You who gives us the New Moon,
> Symbol of new beginnings and illumination.
> Blessed are You,
> As we start again,
> As we celebrate
> the gift of receiving dreams,
> the challenge of seeking wisdom in their interpretation.

## Reflection and Discussion

Invite participants to reflect privately on the past month, noting memorable experiences and dreams that have lingered in their memories. Introduce a discussion of dreams with a few questions:

- What kinds of dreams do you tend to remember?
- How do you find that dreams are meaningful?
- How do you deal with a bad dream?
- What do you think Judaism has to say about dreams?
- Have you ever found guidance in a dream?

*Sharing dreams takes bravery, but it also offers rewards. In fact, sometimes having a dream to share makes it easier to share our feelings. (For example, it can be hard to reveal when you're really scared about something, but if you can say "I had a scary dream" to a friend, it feels as if you've hung onto some privacy.) Friends can sometimes turn out to be our best dream interpreters. Just as friends can offer fresh perspectives on our social situations, they can also offer new perspectives on our dreams and help us find more focus in our lives.*

*Even when our friends have trouble deciphering the symbols of our dreams, if they know what's going on in our lives and know us well enough, they can help us recognize the direction in which our dreams are pointing us.*

*By discussing our dreams with friends, we are less alone. Dreaming becomes an opportunity to engage a friend in the process of understanding our emotions, our thoughts, and our inner voices.*

## Study

Study the ritual practice *hatavat chalom,* making a troubling dream better, in the presence of a dream court of three friends (see p. 66). Ask four volunteers to enact it. Discuss why the ritual may have been developed in this way and imagine how the experience of actually performing the ritual might be transformative for someone having a bad dream.

For girls: Learn about the three-part Jewish bedtime ritual (see pp. 40–46). Learn the Angels' Prayer (see p. 45) in English and Hebrew, and practice singing it.

## Action

Invite participants to write down a dream they've had that has been important to them. After the women have had enough time to write, encourage them to share their dreams. You or the designated facilitator will need to decide whether you wish to encourage others to offer their reactions to the dreams or whether it is better for the group to sit in silent witness. (Some dreams are so weighty or so expressive of vulnerability that the only proper response is a truly respectful, witnessing silence.)

For girls: Prepare a table with arts and crafts materials (paper, markers, scissors, a hole punch, glitter, string, ribbon, old magazines, glue, scraps of wrapping paper, etc.). Make available copies of quotes about dreams offered throughout this book as well as some of your favorite dream interpretations found in the Talmud (see pp. 29–31). Using the materials, each girl can create either her own cover for a *sefer chalomot* or a hanging for her bedroom on which she can write the Angels' Prayer.

## Closing

Bless the New Moon, saying together:

Blessing the New Moon at the proper time,
We have welcomed the *Shekhinah,* the presence of the Divine.
As this New Moon begins,
May we and the ones we love be renewed,
With life, peace, joy, gladness, and illuminating dreams.
Amen.

# chapter nine

# Seeking Healing through Dreams

Researchers in complementary and alternative medicine have been searching for scientific evidence that confirms what people in diverse faith traditions have long held as a firm conviction needing no proof: that prayers, both those said for oneself and those said for others (called intercessory prayer), can play a role in healing. In the Talmud, we learn that a prayer for healing need not only be a spoken prayer. It can be the prayerful presence of someone who visits a sick person, offering friendship, love, empathy, and the physical connection of touch, which raises up the sick person out of isolation and despair and brings healing.

Dreams, too, can be a kind of prayer that encourages healing. This is the contention of Larry Dossey, M.D., author of *Healing Words: The Power of Prayer and the Practice of Medicine.* Dr. Dossey, in his study of mystical traditions, has observed, "A state of prayerfulness has infiltrated not just the conscious mind but the unconscious as well, including sleep and dreams."[1] That is, we who are accustomed to praying are probably praying unconsciously in our dreams. In fact, Dr. Dossey believes that the most effective prayer may be the dream prayer that occurs when we are neither inhibited nor distracted by the state of being awake. In dream prayer, we experience deep connections with God, as well as awe, insight, unity, and wholeness. If we accept the complementary and alternative medicine research, which claims that visualizing wellness, both for oneself and for others, can encourage healing, then visualizing wellness in a dream might also be a means to healing.

A Jewish perspective on healing endorses looking into any safe modality of treatment that offers the possibility of bringing comfort or cure. If dreams of wholeness for oneself or others can be understood as prayers for healing that can actually bring healing, then beckoning such dreams into your life would be consistent with Jewish healing beliefs.

If you desire to have healing dreams for yourself or others, you might offer this meditation (based on traditional healing prayers) before bedtime:

### A Prayer for Healing Dreams

*Heal us, Source of Healing, Source of Blessing of our*
*ancestors, and we shall be healed. Bring us a complete*
*healing of body and spirit, for You are a true*
*and compassionate Healer.*
*I am prepared and ready for dreams of healing. May*
*it be your will, Master of Dreams, who blesses us*
*with angelic messengers of healing, to bring dreams*
*of healing blessings for (name those who are ill).*
*Blessed are You, Healer of all.*

Do not expect that you will necessarily recall your healing dream as you might recall (and then subject to analysis) other kinds of incubated dreams. Dr. Dossey claims there is anecdotal evidence indicating that "the prayer for healing has originated in the unconscious mind during sleep but is not associated with a remembered dream."[2] Rather, permit yourself to accept that through articulating your hope for healing, you have offered dream prayers for healing whether you recall them or not.

Jewish tradition also encourages attending to the healing instructions that come in dreams. Although you should not avoid a prescribed treatment or engage in a dangerous one because of a dream, you should still heed the advice and caution a healing dream provides.

*(Rabbi Hayyim Vital recalls this dream he once heard:)*

*That year my brother Rabbi Moses became ill and my teacher of blessed memory told me in a dream that I should concentrate on him when I recite the prayer "Heal us" [and concentrate] on the words "Who heals the sick of His people Israel" because "Heals the Sick" in gematria (Jewish numerology) adds up to 288 sparks, from which emanate disease. I should concentrate that these 288 should be repaired and sweetened and through this, healing will come to the sick.*

Rabbi Hayyim Vital[3]

chapter ten
# Practices for Mourning

The process of grieving after the death of a loved one is carefully scripted in Jewish tradition. Many Jews who mourn, even those who might not otherwise choose to follow traditional practices, find solace by following a wise, age-old script of prescribed behaviors at a time in their lives when loss has overturned their notion of how to act, and even who to be.

A mourner can move through the process of grief through dream work as well. Anyone wishing assistance in this kind of grief work is well advised to consult Anne Brener's excellent resource, *Mourning & Mitzvah: A Guided Journal for Walking the Mourner's Path through Grief to Healing.*

## Incubating a Dream That Helps Work through Grief

If you are engaged in the process of grieving, your dreams can assist you as you make peace with the person who has died, address unresolved issues, and help you to go on and reclaim your life. Having "a dream that gives you a clear, unmistakable message about what you are struggling with,"[1] according to Brener, is one way you can care for yourself as you do the work of grieving.

To use dreams as part of the mourning process, prepare for bed by engaging in any of the dream incubation practices (see pp. 62–64) that seem helpful to you. Write down an issue that reflects your challenge in making peace with the deceased.

If you receive a dream that night, write it down in the morning and see whether it connects to the issue that has been on your mind. Then, alone, or with the help of someone wise in dream interpretation, think about the insights it might offer. If you don't recall a dream, try automatic writing. Spend 15 minutes upon waking writing down whatever comes into your head. Read what you have written and reflect on how your words might be avenues for healing.

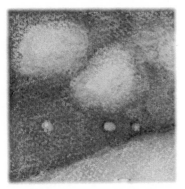

*(In Brener's experience mourning for loved ones, she used the time spent reciting the Mourner's Kaddish, a brief Aramaic prayer in praise of God, as an opportunity to connect with the deceased. She addressed unfinished business she needed to resolve or shared parts of her life. A dream, which she recorded in her journal, documents her experience:)*

## Dream Visitations of the Deceased

Many Jewish mourners engage in the practice of paying attention to the dream visitations of their departed loved ones. They see these appearances of their loved one in their dreams as gifts of connection that reach across the world of the living and the world of the dead. Here are several poignant examples of dream visitations from beyond the grave that have had the power to restore wholeness.

A distinguished woman, beautiful as the sun, approached the top of the ladder. I thought in my heart that it was my mother. She said: "My son, Hayyim, why are you crying? I have heard your tears and have come to help you."

—Hayyim Vital[2]

*Dream: My mother was calling from far, far away, perhaps from another world. The telephone was a model from the time of my birth: black, heavy and with a rotary dial. But its cord was shimmering: translucent, somewhat metallic and pulsating—filled with veins and blood—an umbilical cord, connecting us after her death.... The Kaddish is the silver cord.*

Anne Brener[3]

In the night after the seven days of mourning for Rabbi Abraham, his wife had a dream. She saw a vast hall, and in it thrones, set in a semi-circle. On each throne sat one of the great. A door opened, and one who looked like those others, entered. It was Abraham, her husband. He said, "Friends, my wife bears me a grudge because in my earthly life I lived apart from her. She is right and therefore I must obtain her forgiveness." His wife cried out: "With all my heart I forgive you," and awoke comforted.

—Martin Buber[4]

In the winter of 1955, in her last weeks of life...my mother, dying of cancer, had beautiful dream-visions—in color.... Already beyond calendar time, she could not have known that the last dream she had breath to tell came to her on Christmas Eve.... As a girl in long ago Czarist Russia, she had sternly broken with all observances of organized religion, associating it with pogroms and wars.

(In the mother's dream, three wise men come, but she soon realizes that they are not wise men, but women. They do not wear jeweled robes but coarse clothing, and they do not come with camels, but with farm beasts. In a babble, they speak to her and sing a lullaby.

After her passing, her daughter recalls the lesson of her mother's dream:) "For in the shining cloud of their breaths, a baby lay, breathing universal sounds every human baby makes, sounds out of which are made all the separate languages of the world."

(The mother reflects on her dream:)

"The joy, the reason to believe," my mother said, "the hope for the world, the baby, holy with possibility, that is all of us at birth." And she began to cry, out of the dream, and it's telling now.

(Her daughter later reflects on the gift of her mother's dream and its interpretation.)

"She, who had no worldly goods to leave, yet left to me an inexhaustible legacy. Inherent in it, this heritage of summoning resources to make out of song, food and warmth, expressions of human love—courage, hope, resistance, belief; this vision of universality, before the lessenings, harms, divisions of the world are visited upon it."

—Tillie Olsen[5]

# chapter eleven

# Blessings for Dreaming

The act of blessing our dreams helps us appreciate them even more deeply. Taking the time to bless each moment of life is, for many, the most spiritually engaging practice of Judaism. You needn't know particular Hebrew liturgies or be a member of a congregation. You needn't be erudite in sacred texts or have committed yourself to following the *mitzvot,* the sacred commandments. You only need to be willing to articulate (in words, or in silent feelings) that you are awake to the wonder of every day; willing to see the sacred in all things, all people, all experiences, and all phenomenon; and capable of experiencing gratitude.

There are three kinds of Jewish blessings. Some Jewish blessings were created so long ago and are so familiar to many people that they feel as if they have been recited since the time of Abraham and Sarah. Ritual experts in our own time have created new blessings; only time will tell whether they catch on. Still other blessings are being created spontaneously at each moment by those individuals whose hearts well up with the desire to put their mindful attentiveness into words. For sure, this act of spontaneous blessing has been going on ever since human beings first experienced wonder and gratitude.

The new blessings for dreaming offered below, derived from ancient Jewish sources and traditions, are occasioned by a range of dream experiences.[1] The blessings can inspire you to discover the personal, spontaneous blessings that grow out of the confluence of your own unique dream experiences, your spirit, your sensibilities, your heartfelt needs, and the wise path of ancient Jewish traditions.

### A Blessing of Gratitude for a Dream You Wished For

I have called You from tight places and You answered me with expansiveness. Blessed is the One who has heard my prayers and answered me through my dreams in compassionate ways.

### A Blessing for a Dream That Leaves You Feeling Peaceful

Blessed is the One who creates dreams of peace.

### A Blessing for a Dream That Leaves You Feeling Especially Blessed

Blessed are You, who gifts us with dreams of blessing.

### A Blessing for a Dream That Has Made You Wiser

Blessed is the Source of all illumination and all wisdom,
who guides us in using the knowledge we have acquired
in our dreams for sacred purposes.

### A Blessing for a Dream That Has Raised Your Spirits and Given You Strength

Blessed is the One who provides dreams that restore our spirit and
guide us to move forward with strength and courage.

### A Blessing for a Dream That Has Brought You Healing

Healer of body and spirit, Source of all healing,
You are the Source of this healing dream.

### A Blessing for a Dream That Sets You Off on a Mission

Blessed is the One whose dreams awaken us to goodness, mercy, love,
and compassion. Sustain us as we complete the holy work of
perfecting and repairing the world.

### A Blessing for a Dream That Connects You to Someone Who Has Passed Away

I bless You for the miracle of dreams that restore loving relationships
that transcend the bounds of this life.
Blessed are You who remembers relationships.

### A Blessing for a Dream That Brings You to Repentance and Changes in Your Life

Blessed is the One who gives us dreams that reveal our potential for change and guides us as we turn toward new paths.

### A Blessing for a Dream That Frightens or Mystifies You

Blessed is the One whose presence can be found in all places, even in troubling dreams. Blessed is the One who gives us the ability to distinguish between day and night, the real and the imagined.

### A Blessing Before Interpreting a Dream, Either Yours or Someone Else's

Master of Dreams, bless my efforts to find meaning by guiding me on the path of interpretation with knowledge, understanding, and wisdom.

### A Blessing to Offer for Someone Whose Dream You Have Interpreted

May God bless you and protect you; may God look kindly upon you; may God give you peace.

chapter twelve
# Practices for Linking Your Dreams to Torah

*Recently I (Vanessa) found the key to my dream in Torah. Before moving to a new town for a sabbatical, I was worried about getting settled, finding my way around, and meeting people. In a dream I had, I went to a craft shop and bought mounds of colorless artificial grapes, which I used to decorate a lamp in a room that I had never seen before.*

*To understand what my dream about grapes could teach me, I turned to the passage in Torah about grapes, Num-*

The sages believed that certain dream visions can lead to illuminating interpretations if, soon after you wake up, you recite the most auspicious line in Torah that your dream evokes. Recognizing that the very same dream images could conjure up both positive and negative lines in the Torah, the sages felt it was wise to make positive connections quickly, before one's mind moved to despair. Linking your own dream imagery to positive images in the Torah can be a very powerful source of connection to Jewish tradition. It allows you to extend beyond the boundaries of your own personal narrative and link to the sacred narrative of a people.

In our generation, few are erudite enough to know many Torah passages, positive or negative, that our dreams might evoke. You should feel free to turn to those passages that are familiar to you. Dream about apples, snakes, or trees, and you could turn to the Garden of Eden story. Dream about going on a journey, and you could turn to the story of Abraham setting off. Dream about the desire for a child or pregnancy, and you could turn to any of the stories of the matriarchs who yearned for children: Sarah, Rebecca, Leah, or Rachel. Dream about needing to get out of a bad situation, and you could turn to the story of Moses asking Pharaoh to "let my people go"—and so forth.

Let the story you turn to inspire connections between it and your dream. For example, if you dream about rain or a flood, that could lead you to the Noah story. Reflecting upon the entire story, you may be reminded that after the flood, God's covenant with humanity was renewed. Could you see in your dream signs of renewal or signs of a relationship being restored after a rift?

Below, we offer a sampler of traditional Torah connections evoked by common dream imagery. If you don't see the imagery of your dream here, you can explore either a Bible concordance, which provides all the places in which a particular word might appear, or a Bible translation with commentary that offers an index of topics in the back.

Should your dream imagery lead you to a Torah passage that you don't really understand, you might use this as a sign that you were meant to study that particular part of the Torah and learn what insights it holds for you. You might choose to explore just the particular passage your dream has indicated, or you might expand your exploration to include the verses just before or after it, for in those surrounding verses, you may discover insights that speak to you "where you are." In this kind of dream work that brings the dreamer to the Torah, it is

*bers 13:17 (to find this passage, I used the index of my Hertz commentary on the Torah). Here, the Israelites are anxious about entering the Promised Land they have been journeying toward. To quell their fears, Moses sends out spies to check out the land of Canaan. They come back with reports of a cluster of grapes so large that it takes two men to hold it between them on a pole. Clearly, this is a land of plenty, flowing with milk and honey.*

*I could relate to this. Just as my ancestors were eager to go to the land they had been journeying toward, they were, nonetheless, still scared of the new challenges it could bring. The Torah passage concerning grapes reassured me: it was okay to be anxious about making a move from one place to another.*

*The dream inspired me to be my own spy. I took a trip to the new town a few weeks before we moved, just to scout it out so I might feel less unhinged by the moving process. My "spying trip" calmed me down considerably. On the day I moved in, I already knew where I could find kosher meat and challah, and I was able to zip over to the market to get what I needed in time for the Sabbath! What's more, the colorlessness of the grapes in my dream inspired me to take the advice of a friend who knew were I'd be staying. He had e-mailed to say it was comfortable, but bland, and I'd feel more at home if I brought decorative objects from home. If not for the dream, I probably wouldn't have listened and brought along the knickknacks from home that made me feel so much cozier.*

*(In this dream, in which a Torah scroll appears, Rabbi Tirzah Firestone is directed by her mentor, Leif, to Torah teachings in order to understand what the dream is trying to help her learn as she develops as a spiritual leader.)*

*A few nights later I had a dream.*

*I was in a very old city. A Torah was brought out by old men and carried about on stilts*

more important for you to discover freely how the verses speak to you than it is to engage in rigorous textual analysis. What you want to discover is: "Why has my dream led me to this particular passage?"

These are the traditional links the sages of the Talmud made between their dream imagery and Torah passages. Let the following examples inspire your own links between dreams and Torah.

If you see a river in a dream, turn to this passage: Behold, I will extend prosperity to Jerusalem like a river.... As a mother comforts her child, so I will comfort you. (Isaiah 66:12–13)

If you see a bird in a dream, turn to this passage: Like flying birds, so will God protect Jerusalem. (Isaiah 31:5)

If you see grapes in a dream, turn to this passage: I found Israel as pleasing as grapes in the wilderness. (Hosea 9:10)

If you see a mountain in a dream, turn to this passage: How welcome on the mountain are the footsteps of the herald announcing happiness, good fortune, and victory. (Isaiah 52:7)

If you see a shofar in a dream, turn to this passage: It will be on that day that a great ram's horn will be blown announcing the return of the exile to Jerusalem. (Isaiah 27:13)

If you see a lion in a dream, turn to this passage: God does nothing without having revealed the purpose to the prophets. A lion has roared, who will not fear? (Amos 3:7–8)

If you see an ox, turn to this passage: He (Joseph) has horns like the horns of the wild ox; with them he extends his power over the people, the ends of the earth one and all. (Deuteronomy 33:17)

If you dream of Torah in your dream…you have had a taste of prophecy.

*at an enormous height. There was much weaving and swaying and fear of its falling. Why didn't they simply carry it in their arms, against their chests? I wondered. Then I looked down to find that my own chest had become enormous. I had breasts like Dolly Parton's. I was shocked. My breasts began to let down enormous quantities of milk. "Oh God, what will I do?" I cried.*

*I knew this was an important dream, one in which my unconscious showed its conflict with my new direction. Leif helped me to understand the dream's message. The Torah, the dream was saying, was being held too high above the people, like some strange icon, rather than being held close to the heart. I needed to bring the Torah and her teachings back down to a level that was more human and based in the body. And if I doubted that I had my own feminine wisdom and nourishment from which to draw, the dream came to set me straight. I had plenty. It was coming from inside of me and I'd better get used to it. Come back to what you know, I was being told. You know plenty.*

Rabbi Tirzah Firestone[1]

chapter thirteen
# A Torah Practice
# That Honors Dreamers

This synagogue-based ritual provides a public opportunity to honor people who have been working to better understand their dreams. It would be performed only in those settings in which congregants are comfortable diverging from the traditional structure of the Torah reading service.

On those weeks when Torah portions read in synagogue emphasize the role of dreams (such portions include *Vayyetze* [the dream of Jacob] or *Mikketz* [the dreams of Joseph]), invite dreamers to come up to the Torah for a group *aliyah,* the honor given to people during the service when Torah is read.

The one who is leading the Torah portion of the service invites dreamers to come up to the Torah to say blessings before and after the Torah is chanted. The leader invites the congregation:

> *All who have been attending to their dreams and seeking to interpret them are invited to come up to the Torah for a group aliyah when we read the passages about dreams. When you come up for the dreamers' aliyah, let the melody of the Torah chanting float over you, like a*

*dream. Listen for the word* chalom, *"dream," as it is
chanted, and know that this passage is also about you,
and the wisdom held within your own dreams and
their interpretations. If you are working toward a better
understanding of your dreams, use this as an opportunity to strengthen your resolve to stick with the process
and to celebrate the insights that have come your way.*

Those who have chosen to come up to the Torah chant
together the traditional blessing before the Torah is read:

בָּרְכוּ אֶת יהוה הַמְּבֹרָךְ.
בָּרוּךְ יהוה הַמְּבֹרָךְ לְעוֹלָם וָעֶד.

בָּרוּךְ אַתָּה יהוה אֱלֹהֵינוּ מֶלֶךְ הָעוֹלָם,
אֲשֶׁר בָּחַר בָּנוּ מִכָּל הָעַמִּים
וְנָתַן לָנוּ אֶת תּוֹרָתוֹ.
בָּרוּךְ אַתָּה יהוה, נוֹתֵן הַתּוֹרָה.

*Barkhu et Adonai hamevorakh.*
*Barukh Adonai hamevorakh l'olam va'ed.*

*Barukh ata Adonai, Eloheinu Melekh Ha'olam, asher bachar
banu mi'kol ha'amim, v'natan lanu et Torahto.*
*Barukh ata Adonai, noten Hatorah.*

Blessed are You, Source of Blessing. Blessed are You forever.

Blessed are You, Lord our God, Sovereign of the Universe, who
has chosen us among all peoples by giving us your Torah. Blessed
are you, God, who gives the Torah.

When the Torah has been chanted, the leader says:

*As you and the others chant the traditional blessing
marking the completion of a passage, keep in mind the
Talmudic teaching that advises patience for dreamers:
"One should wait the fulfillment of a good dream for
as much as twenty-two years."*

(Babylonian Talmud, *Brakhot* 55b)

The dreamers recite the concluding blessing:

בָּרוּךְ אַתָּה יהוה אֱלֹהֵינוּ מֶלֶךְ הָעוֹלָם,
אֲשֶׁר נָתַן לָנוּ תּוֹרַת אֱמֶת,
וְחַיֵּי עוֹלָם נָטַע בְּתוֹכֵנוּ.
בָּרוּךְ אַתָּה יהוה, נוֹתֵן הַתּוֹרָה.

*Barukh ata Adonai, Eloheinu Melekh Ha'olam, asher natan lanu
torat emet, v'chayei olam nata b'tokhenu.
Barukh ata Adonai, noten hatorah.*

Blessed are You, Lord our God, Sovereign of the Universe,
who has given us the Torah of truth, planting within us life.
Blessed are You, God, who gives the Torah.

As the dreamers return to their seats, the leader can
encourage the congregants by offering them this kind wish:

"May all your dreams be for the good."

# Notes

## Introduction

1. Sholem Aleichem, *Tevye the Dairyman and the Railroad Stories,* trans. Hillel Halkin (New York: Schocken Books,1996), 50–52.

## 1. The Origin of Dreams

1. Ken Frieden, *Freud's Dream of Interpretation* (Albany: State University of New York Press, 1990), 116.
2. Edmond Jabes, "Mirror and Scarf," in *Gates to the New City: A Treasury of Modern Jewish Tales,* ed. Howard Schwartz (Northvale, New Jersey: Jason Aronson, Inc., 1991), 392.

## 2. Classical Jewish Approaches to Dream Interpretation

1. Ken Frieden, 79–82.
2. Joel Covitz, *Visions in the Night: Jungian and Ancient Dream Interpretation* (Toronto: Inner City Books, 2000), 40.
3. Chaim Potok, *The Chosen* (New York: Simon and Schuster, 1967), 157.
4. Sigmund Freud, *On Dreams,* ed. James Strachey (New York: W. W. Norton, 1990), 108.

## 3. Bedtime Rituals to Help Prepare for Dreaming

1. Morris M. Faierstein, trans., *Jewish Mystical Autobiographies: Book of Visions and Book of Secrets* (New York: Paulist Press, 1999), 97.

## 5. Practices for Interpreting Dreams

1. David Mamet, *Jafsie and John Henry: Essays* (New York: Free Press, 1999), xiii–xiv.
2. Etty Hillesum, *An Interrupted Life and Letters from Westerbork* (New York: Henry Holt, 1996), 61–62.

## 6. Practices for Dream Incubation

1. Joel Covitz, 76.
2. Morris M. Faierstein, 77–78.
3. Joel Covitz, 81.

### 7. Practices for Responding to Nightmares: *Hatavat Chalom*

1. S. Ansky, *The Dybbuk* (New York: Liveright, 1926), 120.
2. Ellen Frankel, *The Five Books of Miriam* (New York: G.P. Putnam's Sons, 1996), 83.
3. Rachel Naomi Remen, *Kitchen Table Wisdom: Stories That Heal* (New York: Riverhead Books, 1997), 97–99.

### 9. Seeking Healing through Dreams

1. Larry Dossey, *Healing Words: The Power of Prayer and the Practice of Medicine* (San Francisco: HarperCollins Publishers, 1993), 70.
2. Ibid., 78.
3. Morris M. Faierstein, 92–93.

### 10. Practices for Mourning

1. Anne Brener, *Mourning & Mitzvah: A Guided Journal for Walking the Mourner's Path through Grief to Healing* (Woodstock, Vt.: Jewish Lights Publishing, 1993), 138.
2. Morris M. Faierstein, 79.
3. Anne Brener, 148.
4. Martin Buber, *Tales of the Hasidim: The Early Masters* (New York: Schocken Books, 1991), 117.
5. Tillie Olsen, "Dream-Vision," in *Shaking Eve's Tree: Short Stories of Jewish Women,* ed. Sharon Niederman (Philadelphia: The Jewish Publication Society, 1990), 122–23.

### 11. Blessings for Dreaming

1. Some of the blessings have been inspired by *The Book of Jewish Sacred Practices: CLAL's Guide to Everyday & Holiday Rituals & Blessings,* edited by Irwin Kula and Vanessa L. Ochs (Woodstock, Vt.: Jewish Lights Publishing, 2001).

### 12. Practices for Linking Your Dreams to Torah

1. Rabbi Tirzah Firestone, *With Roots in Heaven: One Woman's Passionate Journey into the Heart of Her Faith* (New York: Penguin Group, 1998), 249–50.

# Glossary

*aliyah:* Honor given to people during the Torah reading part of the service.

*amidah* (standing): The silent prayer, recited three times a day.

*birkat kohanim:* The priestly blessing.

*Brakhot:* A tractate of the Talmud concerning blessings that includes a lengthy discussion of dreams.

*cheshbon hanefesh:* An account of one's soul, reflection.

*chalom:* A dream.

halakhah: Jewish law.

*Ha'mapil* (The one who casts): The first part of the traditional bedtime prayer, a request for protection in the night.

*hatavat chalom:* A ritual for transforming a bad dream into a good one.

kabbalists: The practitioners of the Jewish mystical tradition.

*Kaddish:* The Aramaic prayer in praise of God, recited in memory of the dead.

*kavannah:* A state of spiritual focus one attempts to achieve while a prayer is said or as a ritual is performed.

*kohanim:* The ancient temple priests and those who trace their ancestry to them.

*Kriyat Sh'ma al hamita:* The traditional bedtime prayer.

*lulav* and *etrog:* The palm branch and citron fruit used in rituals of Sukkot (the Feast of Booths).

*mitzvot* (sing., *mitzvah*): The sacred commandments.

*mikvah:* A ritual bath.

*minhagim* (sing., *minhag*): Jewish customs.

*Mishnah:* The collection of rabbinic commentary on the laws of the Torah, edited in the second century.

*Modeh Ani:* The morning prayer said upon awakening, recited to express gratefulness for the return of one's soul following sleep.

*musaf:* The additional service recited on the Sabbath and holidays.

**Rosh Hashanah:** The Jewish New Year.

**Rosh Chodesh:** The New Moon holiday, which has been revived as a ritual gathering for Jewish women in modernity.

*sefer chalomot:* A dream book.

**Shabbat:** The Sabbath, or day of rest.

*she'elat chalom:* A dream question; the practice of dream incubation.

*Shekhinah:* God's immanent presence.

*shivah:* The seven-day mourning period following a funeral when one stays home and is consoled by friends and family.

*Sh'ma:* The core statement of Jewish belief and loyalty.

**Talmud:** The edited compendium of Jewish law and lore dating back to the period between 200 and 500 C.E.

*tefillin:* Two leather prayer straps and boxes containing texts from the Torah which some wear on their head and arm during the morning prayers.

*teshuvah:* Turning, the possibility of changing one's ways for the better.

**Torah:** The first five books of the Bible, also used to refer to all of Jewish teaching.

**yarmulke:** The skullcap worn as a reminder of God's presence.

**Yom Kippur:** The Day of Atonement.

*Zohar:* Central kabbalistic text, claimed to be written in the second century, but most likely written in the thirteenth century by Moses de Leon.

# Suggestions for Further Reading

Ancient Jewish sources that refer to dreams include the Bible, the Midrash, the Talmud, the *Zohar* and other mystical texts, and the prayer book. Another intriguing source is *The Interpretation of Dreams,* written by Rabbi Solomon Almoli, a sixteenth-century physician and judge who lived in Constantinople.

In this study, we have emphasized the Talmudic passages on dreams. If you have never studied Talmud and are motivated to do so now, think of it as a marvelous document that you have inherited, one created collectively by many of your ancestors. Although there are rigorous traditional methods of Talmud study, we encourage you to approach Talmud as a poem whose meaning you have the honor and the ability to interpret. Open up an English translation of the tractate *Brakhot* (Blessings) in the Babylonian Talmud to any page between 55a and 57a (in some editions, *Brakhot* comes in two volumes, and you'll want to look at the second volume). Notice what jumps out at you, seizes your imagination, or grabs your heart or mind. Look at the text dreamily and ask, "What insights does it open up to me? What associations does it have?" Trust all of your own human instincts and intuitions and your highly developed skill as a reader and interpreter of texts. Translations of the tractate *Brakhot* of the Babylonian Talmud are available in English in editions from Artscroll (the Schottenstein edition), Soncino, and Random House (the Steinsaltz edition). They can be purchased at most Judaica bookshops or found in synagogue and university libraries.

To learn more about dreaming, both in general and from a Jewish perspective, you might wish to consult the following books:

Almoli, Rabbi Shelomo. *Dream Interpretation from Classical Jewish Sources.* Translated by Yaakov Elman. Hoboken, N.J.: KTAV, Inc., 1998.

Bar, Shaul. *A Letter That Has Not Been Read: Dreams in the Hebrew Bible.* Translated by Lenn J. Schramm. Cincinnati: Hebrew Union College Press, 2001.

Barrett, Deirdre. *The Committee of Sleep: How Artists, Scientists, and Athletes Use Dreams for Creative Problem-Solving—and How You Can, Too.* New York: Crown Publishers, 2001.

Bialik, Hayyim Nahman and Yehoshua Hana Ravnitzky, editors. *The Book of Legends-Sefer Ha-Aggadah: Legends from the Talmud and Midrash.* New York: Schocken Books, 1992.

Brener, Anne. *Mourning & Mitzvah: A Guided Journal for Walking the Mourner's Path through Grief to Healing.* Woodstock, Vt.: Jewish Lights Publishing, 1993.

Broner, E. M. *Bringing Home the Light: A Jewish Woman's Handbook of Rituals.* San Francisco: Council Oak Distribution, 1999.

Buber, Martin. *Tales of the Hasidim: The Early Masters.* New York: Schocken Books, 1991.

Bulkeley, Kelly. *Dreams: A Reader on Religious, Cultural, and Psychological Dimensions of Dreaming.* New York: Palgrave Macmillan, 2001.

————. *Visions of the Night: Dreams, Religion, and Psychology.* Albany: State University of New York Press, 1999.

Cooper, Rabbi David A. *The Handbook of Jewish Meditation Practices: A Guide for Enriching the Sabbath and Other Days of Your Life.* Woodstock, Vt.: Jewish Lights Publishing, 2000.

Covitz, Joel. *Visions in the Night: Jungian and Ancient Dream Interpretation.* Toronto: Inner City Books, 2000.

Dossey, Larry. *Healing Words: The Power of Prayer and the Practice of Medicine.* San Francisco: HarperCollins Publishers, 1993.

Faierstein, Morris M., translator. *Jewish Mystical Autobiographies: Book of Visions and Book of Secrets.* New York: Paulist Press, 1999.

Firestone, Rabbi Tirzah. *With Roots in Heaven: One Woman's Passionate Journey into the Heart of Her Faith.* New York: Penguin Group, 1998.

Frankiel, Tamar, and Judy Greenfeld. *Entering the Temple of Dreams: Jewish Prayers, Movements, and Meditations for the End of the Day.* Woodstock, Vt.: Jewish Lights Publishing, 2000.

Freud, Sigmund. *On Dreams*. Edited by James Strachey. New York: W. W. Norton, 1990.

———. *Interpretation of Dreams*. Edited by James Strachey. New York: Barnes and Noble Books, 1994.

Frieden, Ken. *Freud's Dream of Interpretation*. Albany: State University of New York Press, 1990.

Handelman, Susan A. *The Slayers of Moses: The Emergence of Rabbinic Interpretation in Modern Literary Theory*. Albany: State University of New York Press, 1982.

Hillesum, Etty. *An Interrupted Life and Letters from Westerbork*. New York: Henry Holt, 1996.

Jung, C. G. *Memories, Dreams, Reflections*. New York: Vintage Books, 1989.

Kaplan, Connie Cockrell. *Dreams Are Letters from the Soul: Discover the Connections Between Your Dreams and Your Spiritual Life*. New York: Crown Publishers, 2002.

———. *The Woman's Book of Dreams: Dreaming As a Spiritual Practice*. Portland, Oreg.: Beyond Words Publishing Company, 1999.

Remen, Rachel Naomi. *Kitchen Table Wisdom: Stories That Heal*. New York: Riverhead Books, 1997.

Zornberg, Avivah Gottlieb. *Genesis: The Beginning of Desire*. Philadelphia: The Jewish Publication Society, 1995.

# Dream notes

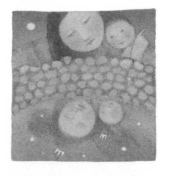

# Dream notes

# Dream notes

# About JEWISH LIGHTS Publishing

People of all faiths and backgrounds yearn for books that attract, engage, educate, and spiritually inspire.

Our principal goal is to stimulate thought and help all people learn about who the Jewish People are, where they come from, and what the future can be made to hold. While people of our diverse Jewish heritage are the primary audience, our books speak to people in the Christian world as well and will broaden their understanding of Judaism and the roots of their own faith.

We bring to you authors who are at the forefront of spiritual thought and experience. While each has something different to say, they all say it in a voice that you can hear.

Our books are designed to welcome you and then to engage, stimulate, and inspire. We judge our success not only by whether or not our books are beautiful and commercially successful, but by whether or not they make a difference in your life.

We at Jewish Lights take great care to produce beautiful books that present meaningful spiritual content in a form that reflects the art of making high quality books. Therefore, we want to acknowledge those who contributed to the production of this book.

*Stuart M. Matlins, Publisher*

PRODUCTION
Tim Holtz, Sara Dismukes & Bridgett Taylor

EDITORIAL
Amanda Dupuis & Emily Wichland

COVER & TEXT DESIGN
Drena Fagen, New York, New York

COVER / TEXT PRINTING & BINDING
Times Publishing, Malaysia

# *Spirituality/Jewish Meditation*

**Aleph-Bet Yoga:** *Embodying the Hebrew Letters for Physical and Spiritual Well-Being*
by *Steven A. Rapp;* Foreword by *Tamar Frankiel & Judy Greenfeld;* Preface by *Hart Lazer*

Blends aspects of hatha yoga and the shapes of the Hebrew letters. Connects yoga practice with Jewish spiritual life. Easy-to-follow instructions, b/w photos. 7 x 10, 128 pp, Quality PB, b/w photos, ISBN 1-58023-162-4 **$16.95**

**The Rituals & Practices of a Jewish Life:** *A Handbook for Personal Spiritual Renewal*
by *Rabbi Kerry M. Olitzky & Rabbi Daniel Judson;* Foreword by *Vanessa L. Ochs;* Illus. by *Joel Moskowitz*

This easy-to-use handbook explains the why, what, and how of ten specific areas of Jewish ritual and practice: morning and evening blessings, covering the head, blessings throughout the day, daily prayer, tefillin, tallit and *tallit katan,* Torah study, kashrut, *mikvah,* and entering Shabbat. 6 x 9, 272 pp, Quality PB, Illus., ISBN 1-58023-169-1 **$18.95**

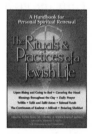    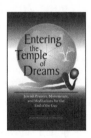 

**Discovering Jewish Meditation:** *Instruction & Guidance for Learning an Ancient Spiritual Practice*
by Nan Fink Gefen  6 x 9, 208 pp, Quality PB, ISBN 1-58023-067-9 **$16.95**

**The Handbook of Jewish Meditation Practices:** *A Guide for Enriching the Sabbath and Other Days of Your Life*
by Rabbi David A. Cooper  6 x 9, 208 pp, Quality PB, ISBN 1-58023-102-0 **$16.95**

**Meditation from the Heart of Judaism:** *Today's Teachers Share Their Practices, Techniques, and Faith*
Ed. by Avram Davis  6 x 9, 256 pp, Quality PB, ISBN 1-58023-049-0 **$16.95**

**The Way of Flame:** *A Guide to the Forgotten Mystical Tradition of Jewish Meditation*
by Avram Davis  4½ x 8, 176 pp, Quality PB, ISBN 1-58023-060-1 **$15.95**

**Minding the Temple of the Soul:** *Balancing Body, Mind, and Spirit through Traditional Jewish Prayer, Movement, and Meditation*
by Tamar Frankiel & Judy Greenfeld  7 x 10, 184 pp, Quality PB, Illus., ISBN 1-879045-64-8 **$16.95**

**Entering the Temple of Dreams:** *Jewish Prayers, Movements, and Meditations for the End of the Day*
by Tamar Frankiel & Judy Greenfeld  7 x 10, 192 pp, Illus., Quality PB, ISBN 1-58023-079-2 **$16.95**

# Life Cycle/Grief/Divorce

### Divorce Is a Mitzvah: *A Practical Guide to Finding Wholeness and Holiness When Your Marriage Dies*

by *Rabbi Perry Netter*; Afterword—"Afterwards: New Jewish Divorce Rituals"—by *Rabbi Laura Geller*

What does Judaism tell you about divorce? This first-of-its-kind handbook provides practical wisdom from biblical and rabbinic teachings and modern psychological research, as well as information and strength from a Jewish perspective for those experiencing the challenging life-transition of divorce. 6 x 9, 224 pp, Quality PB, ISBN 1-58023-172-1 **$16.95**

### Against the Dying of the Light: *A Parent's Story of Love, Loss and Hope*

by *Leonard Fein*

The sudden death of a child. A personal tragedy beyond description. Rage and despair deeper than sorrow. What can come from it? Raw wisdom and defiant hope. In this unusual exploration of heartbreak and healing, Fein chronicles the sudden death of his 30-year-old daughter and reveals what the progression of grief can teach each one of us.
5½ x 8½, 176 pp, HC, ISBN 1-58023-110-1 **$19.95**

### Mourning & Mitzvah, 2nd Ed.: *A Guided Journal for Walking the Mourner's Path through Grief to Healing* *with Over 60 Guided Exercises*

by *Anne Brener, L.C.S.W.*

For those who mourn a death, for those who would help them, for those who face a loss of any kind, Brener teaches us the power and strength available to us in the fully experienced mourning process. Revised and expanded.
7½ x 9, 304 pp, Quality PB, ISBN 1-58023-113-6 **$19.95**

### Grief in Our Seasons: *A Mourner's Kaddish Companion*

by *Rabbi Kerry M. Olitzky*

A wise and inspiring selection of sacred Jewish writings and a simple, powerful ancient ritual for mourners to read each day, to help hold the memory of their loved ones in their hearts. Offers a comforting, step-by-step daily link to saying Kaddish.
4½ x 6½, 448 pp, Quality PB, ISBN 1-879045-55-9 **$15.95**

    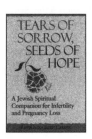 

**Tears of Sorrow, Seeds of Hope:** *A Jewish Spiritual Companion for Infertility and Pregnancy Loss*
by Rabbi Nina Beth Cardin   6 x 9, 192 pp, HC, ISBN 1-58023-017-2 **$19.95**

**A Time to Mourn, A Time to Comfort:** *A Guide to Jewish Bereavement and Comfort*
by Dr. Ron Wolfson   7 x 9, 336 pp, Quality PB, ISBN 1-879045-96-6 **$18.95**

**When a Grandparent Dies:** *A Kid's Own Remembering Workbook for Dealing with Shiva and the Year Beyond*
by Nechama Liss-Levinson, Ph.D.   8 x 10, 48 pp, HC, Illus., 2-color text, ISBN 1-879045-44-3 **$15.95**   **For ages 7–13**

# Healing/Wellness/Recovery

**Jewish Paths toward Healing and Wholeness:** *A Personal Guide to Dealing with Suffering*
by *Rabbi Kerry M. Olitzky*; Foreword by *Debbie Friedman*

Why me? Why do we suffer? How can we heal? Grounded in personal experience with illness and Jewish spiritual traditions, this book provides healing rituals, psalms and prayers that help readers initiate a dialogue with God, to guide them along the complicated path of healing and wholeness. 6 x 9, 192 pp, Quality PB, ISBN 1-58023-068-7 **$15.95**

**Healing of Soul, Healing of Body:** *Spiritual Leaders Unfold the Strength & Solace in Psalms*
Ed. by *Rabbi Simkha Y. Weintraub*, CSW, for The National Center for Jewish Healing

For those who are facing illness and those who care for them. Inspiring commentaries on ten psalms for healing by eminent spiritual leaders reflecting all Jewish movements make the power of the psalms accessible to all.
6 x 9, 128 pp, Quality PB, Illus., 2-color text, ISBN 1-879045-31-1 **$14.95**

**Jewish Pastoral Care:** *A Practical Handbook from Traditional and Contemporary Sources*
Ed. by *Rabbi Dayle A. Friedman*

Gives today's Jewish pastoral counselors practical guidelines based in the Jewish tradition.
6 x 9, 464 pp, HC, ISBN 1-58023-078-4 **$35.00**

**Twelve Jewish Steps to Recovery:** *A Personal Guide to Turning from Alcoholism & Other Addictions—Drugs, Food, Gambling, Sex . . .* by Rabbi Kerry M. Olitzky & Stuart A. Copans, M.D.; Preface by Abraham J. Twerski, M.D.; "Getting Help" by JACS Foundation  6 x 9, 144 pp, Quality PB, ISBN 1-879045-09-5 **$14.95**

**One Hundred Blessings Every Day:** *Daily Twelve Step Recovery Affirmations, Exercises for Personal Growth & Renewal Reflecting Seasons of the Jewish Year*
by Rabbi Kerry M. Olitzky  4½ x 6½, 432 pp, Quality PB, ISBN 1-879045-30-3 **$14.95**

**Recovery from Codependence:** *A Jewish Twelve Steps Guide to Healing Your Soul*
by Rabbi Kerry M. Olitzky  6 x 9, 160 pp, Quality PB, ISBN 1-879045-32-X **$13.95**

**Renewed Each Day:** *Daily Twelve Step Recovery Meditations Based on the Bible*
by Rabbi Kerry M. Olitzky & Aaron Z. *Vol. I: Genesis & Exodus; Vol. II: Leviticus, Numbers and Deuteronomy*
*Vol. I:* 6 x 9, 224 pp, Quality PB, ISBN 1-879045-12-5 **$14.95**
*Vol. II:* 6 x 9, 280 pp, Quality PB, ISBN 1-879045-13-3 **$14.95**

# Children's Spirituality

## Cain & Abel
### *Finding the Fruits of Peace* AWARD WINNER!
by *Sandy Eisenberg Sasso*; Full-color illus. by *Joani Keller Rothenberg*

A sensitive recasting of the ancient tale shows we have the power to deal with anger in positive ways. Provides questions for kids and adults to explore together.
9 x 12, 32 pp, HC, Full-color illus., ISBN 1-58023-123-3  **$16.95  For ages 5 & up**

"Editor's Choice"—American Library Association's *Booklist*

## For Heaven's Sake by *Sandy Eisenberg Sasso*; Full-color illus. by *Kathryn Kunz Finney* AWARD WINNER!
Everyone talked about heaven, but no one would say what heaven was or how to find it. So Isaiah decides to find out.
9 x 12, 32 pp, HC, Full-color illus., ISBN 1-58023-054-7  **$16.95  For ages 4 & up**

## God Said Amen by *Sandy Eisenberg Sasso*; Full-color illus. by *Avi Katz* AWARD WINNER!
Inspiring tale of two kingdoms: one overflowing with water but without oil to light its lamps; the other blessed with oil but no water to grow its gardens. The kingdoms' rulers ask God for help but are too stubborn to ask each other. Shows that we need only reach out to each other to find God's answer to our prayers.
9 x 12, 32 pp, HC, Full-color illus., ISBN 1-58023-080-6  **$16.95  For ages 4 & up**

## God in Between by *Sandy Eisenberg Sasso*; Full-color illus. by *Sally Sweetland* AWARD WINNER!
If you wanted to find God, where would you look? This magical tale teaches that God can be found where we are: within us and the relationships between us. 9 x 12, 32 pp, HC, Full-color illus., ISBN 1-879045-86-9  **$16.95  For ages 4 & up**

## Noah's Wife: *The Story of Naamah*
by *Sandy Eisenberg Sasso*; Full-color illus. by *Bethanne Andersen*  AWARD WINNER!
Opens religious imaginations to new ideas about the story of the Flood. When God tells Noah to bring the animals onto the ark, God also calls on Naamah, Noah's wife, to save each plant on Earth.
9 x 12, 32 pp, HC, Full-color illus., ISBN 1-58023-134-9  **$16.95  For ages 4 & up**

## But God Remembered: *Stories of Women from Creation to the Promised Land* AWARD WINNER!
by *Sandy Eisenberg Sasso*; Full-color illus. by *Bethanne Andersen*
Vibrantly brings to life four stories of courageous and strong women from ancient tradition; all teach important values through their actions and faith. 9 x 12, 32 pp, HC, Full-color illus., ISBN 1-879045-43-5  **$16.95  For ages 8 & up**

# *Children's Spirituality*

### In Our Image: *God's First Creatures*   AWARD WINNER!
by *Nancy Sohn Swartz*; Full-color illus. by *Melanie Hall*

A playful new twist on the Creation story—from the perspective of the animals. Celebrates the interconnectedness of nature and the harmony of all living things.
9 x 12, 32 pp, HC, Full-color illus., ISBN 1-879045-99-0 **$16.95   For ages 4 & up**

"The vibrantly colored illustrations nearly leap off the page in this delightful interpretation." —*School Library Journal*

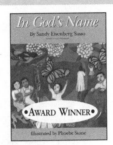

## God's Paintbrush by *Sandy Eisenberg Sasso*; Full-color illus. by *Annette Compton*   AWARD WINNER!
Invites children of all faiths and backgrounds to encounter God openly in their own lives. Wonderfully interactive; provides questions adult and child can explore together at the end of each episode.
11 x 8½, 32 pp, HC, Full-color illus., ISBN 1-879045-22-2 **$16.95   For ages 4 & up**

*Also available:* **A Teacher's Guide: A Guide for Jewish & Christian Educators and Parents**
8½ x 11, 32 pp, PB, ISBN 1-879045-57-5 **$8.95**

**God's Paintbrush Celebration Kit**  9½ x 12, HC, Includes 5 sessions/40 full-color Activity Sheets and Teacher Folder with complete instructions, ISBN 1-58023-050-4 **$21.95**

## In God's Name by *Sandy Eisenberg Sasso*; Full-color illus. by *Phoebe Stone*   AWARD WINNER!
Like an ancient myth in its poetic text and vibrant illustrations, this award-winning modern fable about the search for God's name celebrates the diversity and, at the same time, the unity of all people.
9 x 12, 32 pp, HC, Full-color illus., ISBN 1-879045-26-5 **$16.95   For ages 4 & up**

## What Is God's Name? (A Board Book) An abridged board book version of award-winning *In God's Name.*
5 x 5, 24 pp, Board, Full-color illus., ISBN 1-893361-10-1 **$7.95   For ages 0–4** A SKYLIGHT PATHS Book

## The 11th Commandment: *Wisdom from Our Children* by *The Children of America*   AWARD WINNER!
"If there were an Eleventh Commandment, what would it be?" Children of many religious denominations across America answer this question—in their own drawings and words. "A rare book of spiritual celebration for all people, of all ages, for all time."—*Bookviews* 8 x 10, 48 pp, HC, Full-color illus., ISBN 1-879045-46-X **$16.95   For all ages**

# *Children's Spirituality*

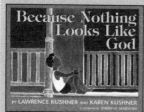

## Because Nothing Looks Like God
by *Lawrence* & *Karen Kushner*; Full-color illus. by *Dawn W. Majewski*

### MULTICULTURAL, NONDENOMINATIONAL, NONSECTARIAN

What is God like? The first collaborative work by husband-and-wife team Lawrence and Karen Kushner introduces children to the possibilities of spiritual life. Real-life examples of happiness and sadness—from goodnight stories, to the hope and fear felt the first time at bat, to the closing moments of life—invite us to explore, together with our children, the questions we all have about God, no matter what our age.

11 x 8½, 32 pp, HC, Full-color illus., ISBN 1-58023-092-X **$16.95  For ages 4 & up**

*Also available: Teacher's Guide,* 8½ x 11, 22 pp, PB, ISBN 1-58023-140-3  **$6.95  For ages 5–8**

## Where Is God?
## What Does God Look Like?
## How Does God Make Things Happen? (Board Books)
by *Lawrence* & *Karen Kushner*; Full-color illus. by *Dawn W. Majewski*

Gently invites children to become aware of God's presence all around them. Three board books abridged from *Because Nothing Looks Like God* by Lawrence and Karen Kushner.
Each 5 x 5, 24 pp, Board, Full-color illus. **$7.95  For ages 0–4**  SKYLIGHT PATHS Books

## Sharing Blessings: *Children's Stories for Exploring the Spirit of the Jewish Holidays*
by *Rahel Musleah* & *Rabbi Michael Klayman*; Full-color illus.

What is the spiritual message of each of the Jewish holidays? How do we teach it to our children? Through stories about one family's life, *Sharing Blessings* explores ways to get into the *spirit* of thirteen different holidays.
8½ x 11, 64 pp, HC, Full-color illus., ISBN 1-879045-71-0  **$18.95  For ages 6 & up**

## The Book of Miracles: *A Young Person's Guide to Jewish Spiritual Awareness*   AWARD WINNER!
by *Lawrence Kushner*

Introduces kids to a way of everyday spiritual thinking to last a lifetime. Kushner, whose award-winning books have brought spirituality to life for countless adults, now shows young people how to use Judaism as a foundation on which to build their lives.

6 x 9, 96 pp, HC, 2-color illus., ISBN 1-879045-78-8  **$16.95  For ages 9 & up**

**H**i, everyone! It's your favorite friend and captain, Frankie! Floyd and I are going on a trip to Tree Fort Island today. Join us for a fantastic adventure!

See these coins? Every time you learn something new, you get one of these stickers to put in your money sack. When you finish each section, you'll get a treasure sticker to put on your Certificate of Completion at the end of the book.

See this picture of me? When you see this picture on the page, it means I'm there to give you a little help. Just look for **Frankie's Facts**.

Are you ready? Raise the sails, we're off!

## Frankie's Facts

There are 21 **consonants** in the alphabet. A consonant is any letter that is not a vowel.

Ahoy! We're sailing to Tree Fort Island. Can you help us get there? **Say the picture name on each ship. Circle the consonant that stands for the beginning sound.**

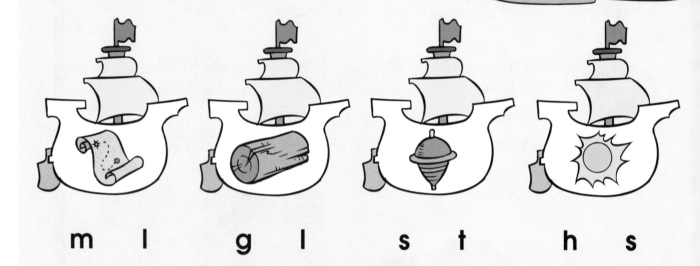

m  l          g  l          s  t          h  s

We're almost there! Now circle the consonant that stands for the ending sound in each picture name below.

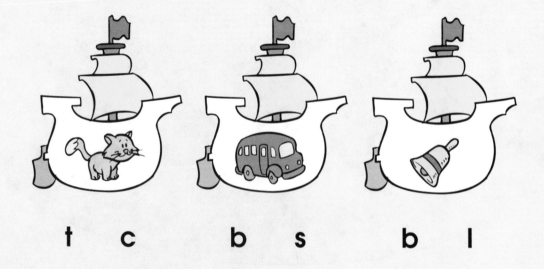

t  c          b  s          b  l

Let's play in the leaves around the tree fort!
**Say the picture name in each leaf. Write the missing beginning or ending consonant on the line.**

\_\_\_ose

fro\_\_\_

\_\_\_ite

fo\_\_\_

\_\_\_ate

bea\_\_\_

soc\_\_\_

**Great job! Put your coin sticker in your money sack and jump ahead to the next level.**

Help me find some acorns for a tree fort snack!

**Say the picture name in each acorn. Write the missing beginning or ending letter on the line.**

\_\_\_oat

\_\_\_all

cra\_\_\_

be\_\_\_

\_\_\_orm

\_\_\_esk

\_\_\_an

tu\_\_\_

Look at the ladders to the tree fort!
Help us climb up.
**Circle the picture whose name has the beginning or ending consonant shown at the bottom of the ladder. Then write the letters on the lines to finish the words.**

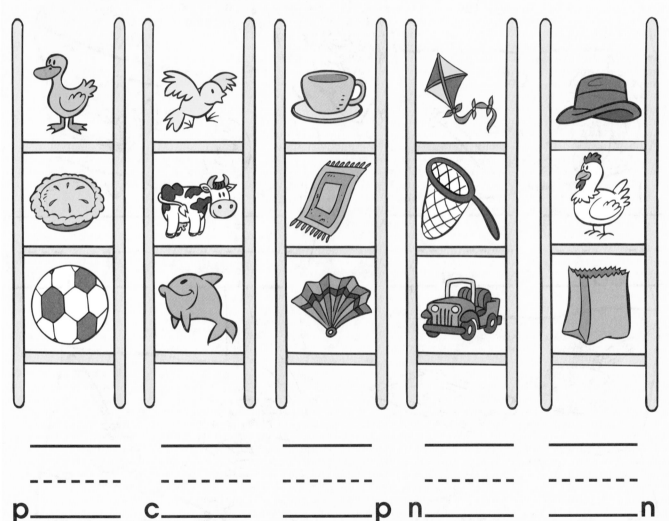

p_____   c_____   _____p   n_____   _____n

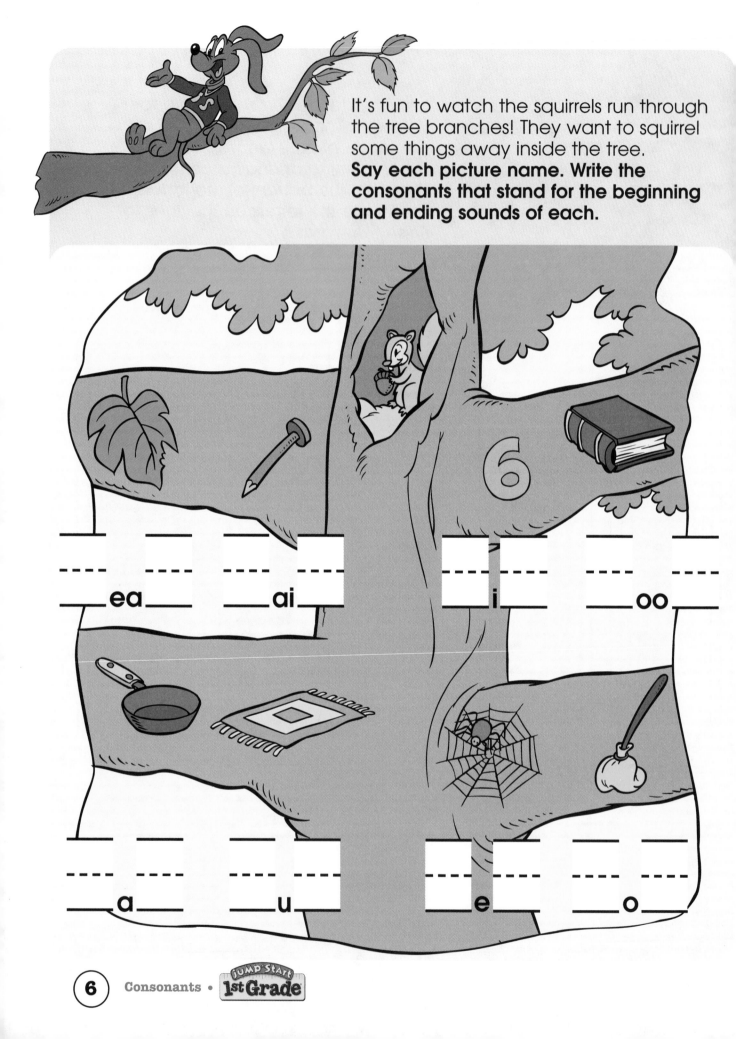

It's fun to watch the squirrels run through the tree branches! They want to squirrel some things away inside the tree.

**Say each picture name. Write the consonants that stand for the beginning and ending sounds of each.**

___ ea ___        ___ ai ___        ___ i ___        ___ oo ___

___ a ___        ___ u ___        ___ e ___        ___ o ___

It's lunchtime! Let's fill our bowls.
**Look at the letter on each bowl. Draw a line to the picture word it completes. Then write the letter on the line.**

 g

 n

 d

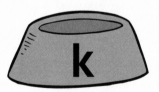 k

 t

mil_____

eg_____

cor_____

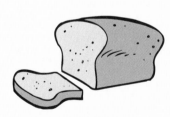
brea_____

nu_____

**Great! Put your coin sticker in your money sack and jump ahead.**

I'm watching birds. You can, too!
Help each bird find its nest.
**Say the name of the picture in each nest. Then find a bird that matches the beginning sound. Draw a line to connect them. Then write the word on the line. Circle the consonant that makes the beginning sound.**

z

v

v

j

j

I've created a secret code for us to use on Tree Fort Island!
Draw a line from the pictures to the correct words. Then write the letter that starts each word.

___ ---- ___ipper

___ ---- ___o-yo

___ ---- ___eep

___ ---- ___ase

Now use the code to crack the secret message! Look at the letter next to each beginning consonant in the secret code box. Each consonant you wrote has a secret letter match. Write the matching letters in order on the lines below.

SECRET CODE
z = b
y = a
j = r
v = k

___ ___ ___ ___
---- ---- ---- ----
___ ___ ___ ___

What do dogs and trees have in common?

_____
- - - - - - - - - - - - - - - - - - - - - - - -
We both have a _____!

**Excellent job! Put your coin sticker in your money sack and jump ahead.**

Consonants    9

What can you see inside the tree fort?
**Look at the words in the word box. Put an X on every word you can find in the picture. Then sort them all by their beginning consonants.**

| | | | | | |
|---|---|---|---|---|---|
| bird | juice | milk | leaf | bed | pan |
| book | zoo | pail | fox | flag | bus |
| yo-yo | light | mask | door | bear | |
| drum | fan | pillow | map | fork | |

Words that begin with **m** or **l**

map

leaf

Words that begin with **b** or **d**

Words that begin with **p** or **f**

Words that begin with **j**, **z**, or **y**

**Nice job! Place your goblet sticker on your Certificate of Completion and jump ahead.**

## Frankie's Facts

The letters **a**, **e**, **i**, **o**, and **u** are **vowels**. Vowels between two consonants usually make a **short** sound. The short vowel sounds are **a** as in c**a**t, **e** as in n**e**t, **i** as in f**i**sh, **o** as in b**o**x, and **u** as in r**u**g.

I am making special tree fort hats. **Say the picture name on each hat. Circle the letter that stands for its short vowel sound.**

*Whee!* Swinging from the tree fort is fun!

**Say the vowel name under each pair of pictures. Circle the picture in each pair with that vowel sound.**

### short e

### short a

### short i

### short o

### short u

**Way to go! Put your coin sticker in your money sack and jump ahead.**

Short Vowels (13)

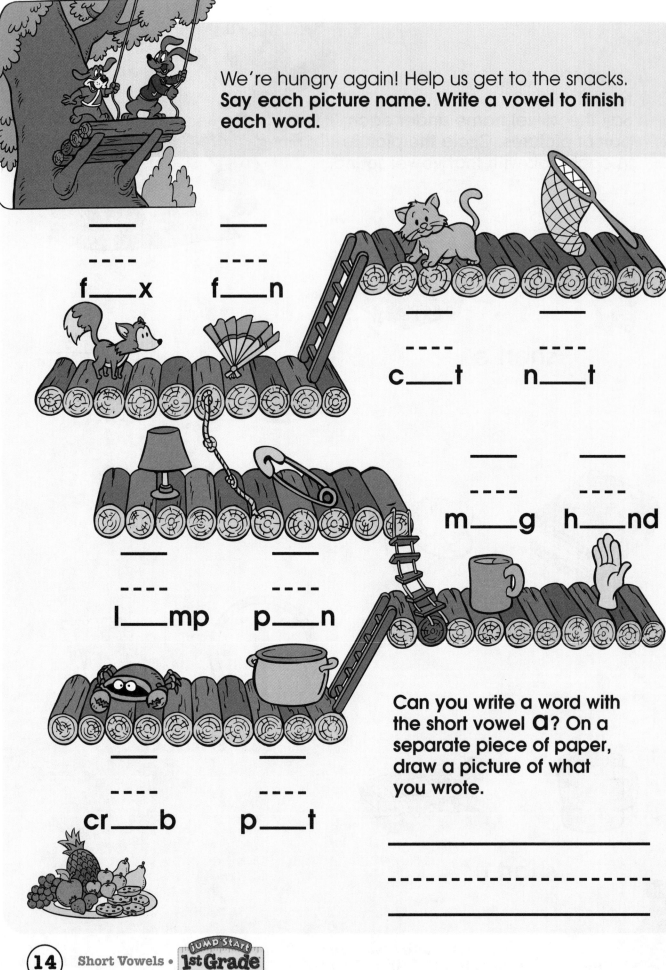

We're hungry again! Help us get to the snacks. **Say each picture name. Write a vowel to finish each word.**

f___x     f___n

c___t     n___t

m___g     h___nd

l___mp     p___n

cr___b     p___t

Can you write a word with the short vowel **a**? On a separate piece of paper, draw a picture of what you wrote.

_____

- - - - - - - - - - - - - - - - - - - - - - -

_____

I'm watching some birds hatch.
You can watch, too!
**Say the picture name on each egg.
Then fill in the short vowels to finish
each word.**

1. s___ck

2. h___t

3. b___g

4. r___ck

5. fr___g

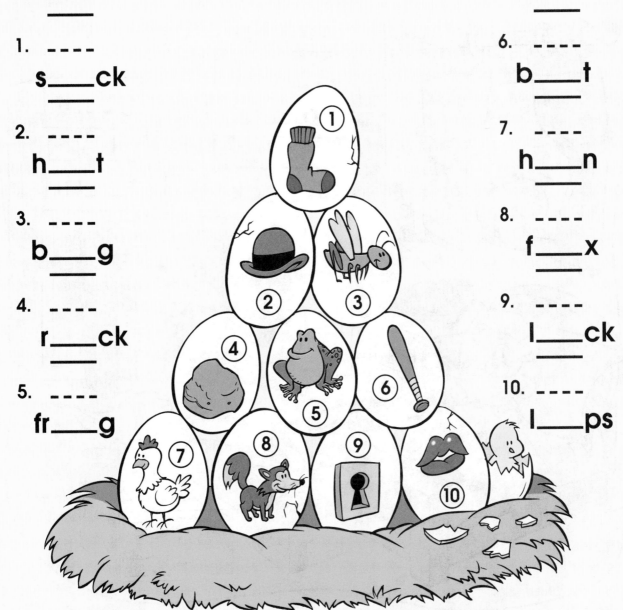

6. b___t

7. h___n

8. f___x

9. l___ck

10. l___ps

**Can you write a word with the short vowel O?
On a separate piece of paper, draw a picture
of what you wrote.**

Floyd is cleaning the tree fort. Can you help him put some things away?

**Write the vowel i to complete each word. Then draw a line to the matching picture.**

sh___p

p___g

ch___ck

g___ft

f___sh

Can you write a word with the short vowel **i**?
On a separate piece of paper, draw a picture
of what you wrote.

- - - - - - - - - - - - - - -

Floyd is climbing trees. You can, too!
Say the name of each picture. Write the missing vowel to complete
that word. Then write the words with short vowel **u** and short vowel
**e** in the box.

b____s

dr____m

sl____d

p____n

b____ll

b____g

| short u | short e |
|---|---|
| | |

Terrific climbing! Put your coin sticker
in your money sack and jump ahead.

**Short Vowels** **17**

Will you help me fix up the tree fort?
**Say each picture name and write the
missing vowel. One picture name on
each table has a short vowel. Circle it.**

__ __
----
m__t

__ __
----
r__ke

__ __
----
b__ne

__ __
----
c__p

__ __
----
b__ll

__ __
----
k__te

Acorns are falling on me! Help!
Circle and write the word that names the picture. Then put an X on the word if it makes a short vowel sound.

pine    pin

------------------------

pan    pane

------------------------

bead    bed

------------------------

bone    coat

------------------------

cat    cake

------------------------

**You did it! Put your coin sticker in your money sack and jump ahead.**

Come on! Let's go on a short vowel nature walk!

**Follow the arrows along the path. Say each picture name. Write the missing vowel to finish each word. Keep going until you reach the lake!**

START

___
----
___gg

___
----
fr___g

___
----
f___x

___
----
s___n

___
----
r___ck

_ _ _ _
__ck

_
_ _ _ _
c__t

_
_ _ _ _
b__t

_
_ _ _ _
n__st

_
_ _ _ _
st__ck

_
_ _ _ _
m__p

FINISH

Stupendous! Place your scepter sticker on
your Certificate of Completion and jump ahead.

Review 21

# Frankie's Facts

**Long vowels** say their name. The long vowel sounds are **a** as in c**a**ke, **e** as in f**ee**t, **o** as in r**o**pe, **i** as in d**i**me, and **u** as in c**u**te.

We're swinging on a tire swing!
**Say each picture name. Then add long vowels to complete each word.**

___ce          c___ke

f_____t          r___se          g___te

b_____          k___te          c___ne

Help us keep swinging!
**Draw a line from each picture to the tire with the same vowel sound.**

long
a

long
e

long
o

long
u

**Super job! Put your coin sticker in your money sack and jump ahead.**

Long Vowels **23**

# Frankie's Facts

Sometimes the letter **e** is silent in words that have a long vowel sound, like c**a**p**e**.

Let's see what we find when we look through my binoculars.
**Write the missing letters to finish the long a words I see.**

___ ___ ___ ___
___ ___a ___es

___ ___
___a ___e

___ ___ ___
___ ___a___e

___ ___ ___
___ ___a___e

___ ___ ___
___ ___a ___e

Can you write another word that has the long **a** sound? _____

Help me make silent **e** masks in the tree fort!
**Circle the word that names the picture. Then write the word on the line.**

mile
smile
mill

_____

- - - - - - - - - - - -

_____

prize
pies
rise

_____

- - - - - - - - - - - -

_____

slid
lid
slide

_____

- - - - - - - - - - - -

_____

five
have
hive

_____

- - - - - - - - - - - -

_____

kite
kit
tie

_____

- - - - - - - - - - - -

_____

dim
dime
dome

_____

- - - - - - - - - - - -

_____

**Can you write another word that has the long i sound?**

- - - - - - - - - - - - - - - - - - - - - - - - -

_____

Come and watch the stars with us!
**Read the words in the box. Then look at the pictures in the stars. Pick the word that goes in each sentence and write it on the line.**

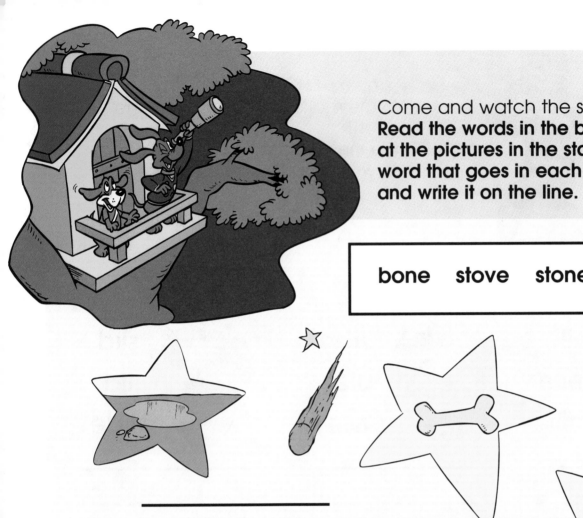

| bone | stove | stone | hose |

_____

The _____ is by the lake.

The _____ is for a dog.

You can get water from a _____.

Dad cooks dinner on a _____.

**Can you write another word that has the long O sound?**
_____

Look at all the cloud shapes!
Say the picture name in each cloud.
Color in the clouds with pictures whose
names have a long **U** sound. Then
write the vowels to finish each word.

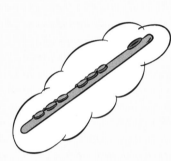

fl__t__          pl__n__          m__l__          c__b__

f__v__          t__b__          J__n__          wh__l__

**Fantastic! Put your coin sticker in
your money sack and jump ahead.**

Long Vowels    **27**

## Frankie's Facts

Vowels that have a **consonant** after them are usually short. Vowels that are followed by a **consonant** and a **silent e** usually make a long sound.

cap            cape

We're at the Tree Fort Island beach! **Say the name of each picture and write that word on the line. If the word has a short vowel, color the shell red. If the word has a long vowel, color the shell blue.**

| globe | lamp | bone |
|-------|------|------|
| frog | skates | cake |

Help Floyd plant flowers!
**Use these letters to make words with long vowel sounds.**

h  k  e

___
- - - -
___ole

___
- - - -
cut___

___
- - - -
ma___e

___
- - - -
___ite

**How many words can you think of that rhyme with the word "gate"?**

**Excellent job! Put your coin sticker in your money sack and jump ahead.**

Long Vowels  (29)

Frankie and I are having a party in the tree fort. You're invited, of course!

**Read each word in the box and circle the picture at the party. Only two of these words have a short vowel. Circle those two words in the word box.**

Now, let's play a party game!
**Find the words from the word box in this puzzle. Circle them all.**

cake
game
kite
rose
rug
drink
cheese
plate
vase

| p | l | a | t | e | c |
|---|---|---|---|---|---|
| c | b | d | c | d | h |
| a | e | r | o | s | e |
| k | k | i | t | e | e |
| e | f | n | v | g | s |
| h | i | k | a | a | e |
| r | u | g | s | m | i |
| m | p | s | e | e | u |

**Congratulations! You did it! Place your crown sticker on your Certificate of Completion.**

Review (31)

# Answer Key

PAGE 2 — circle m, l, t, s; t, s, l

PAGE 3 — write r, g, k, x, g, r, k

PAGE 4 — write c, b, b, d, w, d, c, b

PAGE 5 — circle pie, cow, cup, net, hen; write ie, ow, cu, et, he

PAGE 6 — write l/f, n/l, s/x, b/k, p/n, r/g, w/b, m/p

PAGE 7 — draw lines to connect g/egg, n/corn, d/bread, k/milk, t/nut; write k, g, n, d, t

PAGE 8 — draw lines to connect vest/v, juice/j, jam/j, zebra/z, van/v; write zebra, vest *or* van, van *or* vest, jam *or* juice, juice *or* jam; circle z, v, v, j, j

PAGE 9 — draw lines to connect jeep/eep, zipper/ipper, yo-yo/o-yo, vase/ase; write z, y, j, v; write b, a, r, k; write bark

PAGES 10–11 — write X on all words in word box; for m or l words write light, milk, mask; for p or f words write fan, pail, pillow, fox, flag, fork, pan; for b or d words write bird, book, drum, door, bed, bear, bus; for j, z, or y words write yo-yo, juice, zoo

PAGE 12 — circle e, o, a, u, i

PAGE 13 — circle tent, hat, pig, clock, mug

PAGE 14 — write o, a; a, e; u, a; a, i; a, o; answers will vary

PAGE 15 — write o, a, u, o, o, a, e, o, o, i; answers will vary

PAGE 16 — write i five times; answers will vary

PAGE 17 — write (from top) u, u, e, e, e, u; for short u words write drum, bus, bug; for short e words write pen, sled, bell

PAGE 18 — write a, a, o, u, e, i; circle mat, cup, bell

PAGE 19 — circle and write pin, pan, bed, coat, cake; draw an X on pin, pan, bed

PAGES 20–21 — write e, o, u, a, a, e, i, o, u, o, a

PAGE 22 — write i, a, ee, o, a, ee, i, o

PAGE 23 — draw lines to connect rope/long o, rake/long a, feet/long e, mule/long u

PAGE 24 — write sk/t, r/k, pl/n, pl/t, sn/k; answers will vary

PAGE 25 — circle and write smile, prize, slide, hive, kite, dime; answers will vary

PAGE 26 — write stone, bone, hose, stove; answers will vary

PAGE 27 — color clouds with mule, cube; write u/e, a/e, u/e, u/e, i/e, u/e, u/e, a/e

PAGE 28 — write lamp, frog, cake, skates, globe, bone; color shells red with lamp and frog; color shells blue with cake, skates, globe, bone

PAGE 29 — write h, e, k, k; answers will vary

PAGES 30–31 — circle cake, game, kite, rose, rug, drink, cheese, plate, vase in picture; circle the words rug, drink